REENGINEERING
THE CORPORATION

REENGINEERING THE CORPORATION

A MANIFESTO FOR BUSINESS REVOLUTION

MICHAEL HAMMER & JAMES CHAMPY

NICHOLAS BREALEY
PUBLISHING
LONDON

First published in Great Britain by
Nicholas Brealey Publishing Limited in 1993
156 Cloudesley Road
London N1 0EA

First published in Australia by Allen & Unwin in 1993
9 Atchison Street
St. Leonards NSW 2065
Australia

Published by arrangement with
HarperCollins Publishers, Inc., USA

ISBN 1 85788 029 3

British Library Cataloguing-in-Publication Data
A catalogue record for this book is available from the British Library.

National Library of Australia
Cataloguing-in-Publication entry:
Hammer, Michael, 1948–
Reengineering the corporation.
1st ed.
ISBN 1 86373 505 4
1. Organizational change. 2. Corporate reorganizations.
I. Champy, James, 1942– . II. Title.
658.406

Printed and bound by RRD in America

ACKNOWLEDGMENTS

The central thesis of this book—that American corporations must undertake nothing less than a radical reinvention of how they do their work—may strike some as extreme. But for the risk-averse, we hasten to add that our recommendations and conclusions are based on the successes now being realized by a handful of extraordinary organizations. We owe a great deal to these companies and to their far-sighted executives and managers. While credit is due to many people, a few stand out: David Barry of Ford; Bob Stark of Hallmark Cards; Norm Phelps and Pam Godwin of Capital Holdings; Woody Noxon and Al Van De Moere of Eastman Kodak; Chuck McCaig, now of Chubb Insurance; John Martin of Taco Bell; Stephen Israel and Wayne Hoover of IBM Credit; the late Regis Filtz of Bell Atlantic; Ron Compton of Aetna Life & Casualty; and Bruce Marlow of Progressive Insurance. They and their organizations served as the original role models for reengineering.

We also owe a debt of gratitude to the many colleagues and teachers from whom we have learned so much over the years. To list them all would be impossible, but two deserve special mention: Peter Drucker and Tony Athos, whose insights into organizations inform all our work. We also want to thank the many individuals at CSC Index who shared with us their consulting experiences, gathered case material, and helped to bring this book to fruition. Their contributions can be found throughout the book.

We particularly wish to thank the individuals who were invaluable in the process of making this book a reality: Donna Sammons Carpenter, Tom Richman, and Abby Solomon, whose extraordinary editorial skills helped turn an inchoate mass into a coherent narrative; Helen Rees, our literary agent who taught us the "business" of publishing; and Virginia Smith, our editor at HarperBusiness who supported our work at every step.

Finally, our greatest appreciation is reserved for all those people currently helping to make reengineering a reality in their own organizations and advancing our collective understanding of this new age in business.

For my parents, who showed me the path that I follow; for my wife, with whom I travel it; and for my children, whose paths await them.

M. H.

For my wife, Lois, from whom I have learned so much; and for my son, Adam, for whom I have the joy of teaching.

J. C.

CONTENTS

INTRODUCTION

A set of principles laid down more than two centuries ago has shaped the structure, management, and performance of American businesses throughout the nineteenth and twentieth centuries. In this book, we say that the time has come to retire those principles and to adopt a new set. The alternative is for corporate America to close its doors and go out of business.

The choice is that simple and that stark.

American entrepreneurs, executives, and managers created and operated companies that for more than one hundred years met the expanding demand for mass market products and services. American managers and the companies they ran set the performance standard for the rest of the business world. Sadly, that is no longer the case.

The book you are holding describes a conceptually new business model and an associated set of techniques that American executives and managers will have to use to reinvent their companies for competition in a new world.

To reinvent their companies, American managers must throw out their old notions about how businesses should be organized and run. They must abandon the organizational and operational principles and procedures they are now using and create entirely new ones.

The new organizations won't look much like today's corporations, and the ways in which they buy, make, sell, and deliver products and services will be very different. They will be companies designed specifically to operate in today's world and tomorrow's, not institutions carried over from an earlier, glorious, but no longer relevant age.

For two hundred years people have founded and built companies around Adam Smith's brilliant discovery that industrial work should be broken down into its simplest and most basic *tasks*. In the postindustrial business age we are now entering, corporations will be founded and built around the idea of reunifying those tasks into coherent business *processes*.

In this book we demonstrate how existing corporations *can* reinvent themselves. We call the techniques they can use to accomplish this *business reengineering*, and it is to the next revolution of business what the specialization of labor was to the last. America's largest corporations—even the most successful and promising among them—must embrace and apply the principles of business reengineering, or they will be eclipsed by the greater success of those companies that do.

Reengineering isn't another idea imported from Japan. It isn't another quick fix that American managers can apply to their organizations. It isn't a new trick that promises to boost the quality of a company's product or service or shave a percentage off costs. Business reengineering isn't a program to hike worker morale or to motivate the sales force. It won't push an old computer system to work faster. Business reengineering isn't about *fixing* anything.

Business reengineering means starting all over, starting from scratch.

Business reengineering means putting aside much of the received wisdom of two hundred years of industrial management. It means forgetting how work was done in the age of the mass market and deciding how it can best be done now. In business reengineering, old job titles and old organizational arrangements—departments, divisions, groups, and so on—cease to matter. They are artifacts of another age. What matters in reengineering is how we want to organize work today, given the demands of today's markets and the power of today's technologies. How people and companies did things yesterday doesn't matter to the business reengineer.

Reengineering capitalizes on the same characteristics that have traditionally made Americans such great business innovators: individualism, self-reliance, a willingness to accept risk, and a propensity for change. Business reengineering, unlike management philosophies that would have "us" become more like "them," doesn't try to change the behavior of American workers and managers. Instead, it takes advantage of American talents and unleashes American ingenuity.

At the heart of business reengineering lies the notion of *discontinuous thinking*—identifying and abandoning the outdated rules and fundamental assumptions that underlie current business operations. Every company is replete with implicit rules left over from earlier decades: "Customers don't repair their own equipment." "Local warehouses are necessary for good service." "Merchandising decisions are made at headquarters." These rules are based on assumptions about technology, people, and organizational goals that no longer hold. Unless companies change these rules, any superficial reorganizations they perform will be no more effective than dusting the furniture in Pompeii.

How did the concept of business reengineering evolve and how did we develop a methodology for performing it? Nearly ten years ago, we began to notice that a few companies had dramatically improved their performance in one or more areas of their business by radically changing the ways in which they worked. These companies had not changed the businesses they were in; rather, they had significantly altered the processes they followed in those businesses—or even replaced these old processes entirely.

Simultaneously, we were actively engaged in helping some of our clients develop new techniques that would allow them to survive—or even thrive—in an increasingly harsh competitive climate. To do so businesses had to be willing to look across and beyond functional departments to processes—no easy task in corporations that had been for years committed to traditional methods of organization. (By "process," we simply mean a set of activities that, taken together, produce a result of value to a customer—developing a new product, for example.) Almost always, this process change was accompanied by an equally radical change in the shape and character of those parts of the organization that were involved in performing it. It struck us that these companies were achieving dramatic results in part because they would accept nothing less.

We decided to look closer. We wanted to understand why these organizations chose radical change over the less painful remedy of steady, incremental improvements that most businesses usually prefer. We wanted to look for commonalties, if any, in the techniques these companies used to effect their changes. What worked and why? What didn't work and why not? Were these techniques transferable to other organizations in other lines of business? Could they be applied to companies as a whole instead of only to small, discrete parts of an organization?

We discovered that most of the companies we examined that had succeeded in radically changing one or more of their processes had, albeit unknowingly, used a common set of tools and tactics. Conversely, when companies tried but failed to achieve dramatic operating improvements, it was usually for one or more of the same reasons.

We discovered as well that the most impressive companies we examined—those that were aiming for more than a little improvement and succeeding—were asking themselves a different question from that asked by other organizations: They weren't asking "How can we do what we do faster?" or "How can we do what we do better?" or "How can we do what we do at a lower cost?" Instead, they were asking "Why do we do what we do at *all?*"

Why, indeed?

That is the question we began to pose to companies across the United States, and the answers that we received were startlingly revealing. We found that many tasks that employees performed had nothing at all to do with meeting customer needs—that is, creating a product high in quality, supplying that product at a fair price, and providing excellent service. Many tasks were done simply to satisfy the internal demands of the company's own organization.

Little by little, by examining the experiences of many companies, we were able to discern the patterns of actions that led to success and those that didn't, and gradually we could see a set of procedures for effecting radical change take shape. Eventually we gave this set of procedures a name. We called it *business reengineering*. Then we worked out an approach that managers and leaders of other companies can use in their own organizations. Now, dozens of companies are actively engaged in reengineering all or parts of their operations.

Reengineering, we are convinced, can't be carried out in small and cautious steps. It is an all-or-nothing proposition that produces dramatically impressive results. Most companies have no choice but to muster the courage to do it. For many, reengineering is the only hope for breaking away from the ineffective, antiquated ways of conducting business that will otherwise inevitably destroy them.

In this book we offer a powerful argument for business reengineering as the single best hope for restoring the competitive vigor of American businesses. We explore the reasons for reengineering, describe its techniques, and alert readers to the issues they will encounter in a world in which the only successful companies will be those that have drastically changed—reengineered—their business processes.

We also set forth guidelines for initiating, conducting, and following through on the reengineering process in companies whose managements are prescient enough to recognize the need for change and bold enough to undertake it.

Those who follow us from start to finish will learn what we've learned about why most American companies have come to a point at which radical action is required. They will understand how business reengineering works. They will learn, from the experiences of the companies we have studied and assisted, how to succeed in reengineering a business.

This is a book, then, about a future that is already here and a book for people who expect to be part of it. Our book draws upon the experiences of companies that have already learned that the only way to achieve what they must is through business reengineering. But while this book contains many examples, it isn't about anecdotes or stories; it is about ideas. These ideas, we believe, are as important to business *today* as Adam Smith's ideas were to the entrepreneurs and managers of the last two centuries. We believe that the application of the principles of business reengineering will have effects as significant and dramatic as those created by Smith's principles of industrial organization.

As important as we believe this book to be, however, we know that it won't be the last one written about business reengineering. Since *The Wealth of Nations* was published in 1776, countless management manuals have expanded and refined Adam Smith's thoughts. We hope *Reengineering the Corporation: A Manifesto for Business Revolution* will be a seminal book, too—and by no means the final word.

Some time—but not much—remains for American companies to apply the lessons in this book to their own organizations. The problems besetting American business today are urgent. Those companies that act with dispatch on these lessons will be able to compete successfully in a world in which the only predictable constant has already become rapid and relentless change.

THE CRISIS THAT WILL NOT GO AWAY

Not a company in the country exists whose management doesn't say, at least for public consumption, that it wants an organization flexible enough to adjust quickly to changing market conditions, lean enough to beat any competitor's price, innovative enough to keep its products and services technologically fresh, and dedicated enough to deliver maximum quality and customer service.

So, if managements want companies that are lean, nimble, flexible, responsive, competitive, innovative, efficient, customer-focused, and profitable, why are so many American companies bloated, clumsy, rigid, sluggish, noncompetitive, uncreative, inefficient, disdainful of customer needs, and losing money? The answers lie in how these companies do their work and why they do it that way. A few examples illustrate the point that the results companies achieve are often very different from the results that their managements desire.

• A manufacturer we visited has, like many other companies, set a goal of filling customer orders quickly, but this goal is proving elusive. Like most companies in its industry, this company uses a multi-tiered distribution system. That is, factories send finished goods to a central warehouse, the Central Distribution Center (CDC). The CDC in turn ships the products to Regional Distribution Centers (RDCs), smaller warehouses that receive and fill customer orders. One of the RDCs covers the geographical area in which the CDC is located. In fact, the two occupy the same building. Often and inevitably RDCs do not have the goods they need to fill customers' orders. This particular RDC, however, *should* be able to get missing products quickly from the CDC located across the hall, but it doesn't work out that way. That's because even on a rush/ expedite order, the process takes *eleven days:* one day for the RDC to notify the CDC it needs parts; five days for the CDC to check, pick, and dispatch the order; and five days for the RDC to officially receive and shelve the goods, and then pick and pack the customer's order. One reason the process takes so long is that RDCs are rated by the amount of time they take to respond to customer orders, but CDCs are not. Their performance is judged on other factors: inventory costs, inventory turns, and labor costs. Hurrying to fill an RDC's rush order will hurt the CDC's own performance rating. Consequently, the RDC does not even attempt to obtain rush goods from the CDC located across the hall. Instead, it has them air shipped overnight from another RDC. The costs? Air freight bills alone run into the millions of dollars annually; each RDC has a unit that does nothing but work with other RDCs looking for goods; and the same goods are moved and handled more times than good sense would dictate. The RDCs and the CDC are all doing their jobs, but the overall system just doesn't work.

• Often the efficiency of a company's parts comes at the expense of the efficiency of its whole. A plane belonging to a major American airline was grounded one afternoon for repairs at Airport A, but the nearest mechanic qualified to perform the repairs worked at Airport B. The manager at Airport B refused to send the mechanic to Airport A that afternoon, because after completing the repairs the mechanic would have had to stay overnight at a hotel, and the hotel bill would come out of B's budget. So, the mechanic was dispatched to Airport A early the following morning, which enabled him to fix the plane and return home the same day. A multi-million dollar aircraft sat idle, and the airline lost hundreds of thousands of dollars in revenue, but Manager B's budget wasn't hit for a $100 hotel bill. Manager B was neither foolish nor careless. He was doing exactly what he was supposed to be doing: controlling and minimizing his expenses.

• Work that requires the cooperation and coordination of several different departments within a company is often a source of trouble. When retailers return unsold goods for credit to a consumer products manufacturer we know, thirteen separate departments are involved. Receiving accepts the goods, the warehouse returns them to stock, inventory management updates records to reflect their return, promotions determines at what price the goods were actually sold, sales accounting adjusts commissions, general accounting updates the financial records, and so on. Yet no single department or individual is in charge of handling returns. For each of the departments involved, returns are a low-priority distraction. Not surprisingly, mistakes often occur. Returned goods end up "lost" in the warehouse. The company pays sales commissions on *un*sold goods. Worse, retailers do not get the credit that they expect, and they become angry, which effectively undoes all of sales and marketing's efforts. Unhappy retailers are less likely to promote the manufacturer's new products. They also delay paying their bills, and often pay only what *they* think they owe after deducting the value of the returns. This throws the manufacturer's accounts receivable department into turmoil, since the customer's check doesn't match the manufacturer's invoice. Eventually, the manufacturer simply gives up, unable to trace what really happened. Its own estimate of the annual costs and lost revenues from returns and related problems runs to *nine figures*. From time to time, the company's management has attempted to tighten up the disjointed returns process, but it no sooner gets some departments working well than new problems crop up in others.

• Even when the work involved could have a major impact on the bottom line, companies often have no one in charge. As part of the government's approval process for a major new drug, for instance, a pharmaceutical company needed field study results on just one week's dosing of thirty different patients. Obtaining this information took the company *two years*. A company scientist spent four months developing the study and specifying the kind of data to be collected. Actually designing the study took only two weeks, but getting other scientists to review the design took fourteen. Next, a physician spent two months scheduling and conducting interviews in order to recruit other doctors who would identify appropriate patients and actually administer the trial drug. Securing permission from all the hospitals involved took a month, most of which was spent waiting for replies. The physicians administering the one-week dose were paid in advance, so they had no incentive to accelerate their work. Collecting the forms that the doctors filled out took two months. Next, the study administrator sent the forms to data entry, where errors were discovered on about 90 percent of them. Back they went to the protocol designer, who sent them to the study administrator, who returned them to the physicians, who tried to correct the mistakes. As a result of its own field study process (not the government's approval process), the company lost nearly two years' profits, worth millions of dollars, on this drug, as it had on many others. Yet, to this day no one at the company has overall responsibility for getting field studies done.

These are stories taken more or less at random from our experiences; they could be replicated endlessly. These companies are not exceptions; they are the rule. This is not how corporate executives say they want their companies to behave, yet this behavior persists nonetheless. Why?

Corporations do not perform badly because—as some critics have claimed—American workers are lazy and American managements are inept. The American record of industrial and technological accomplishment over the past century is proof enough that managements are not inept and workers do work. The ironic truth is that American companies are now performing so badly precisely because they used to perform so well.

For more than one hundred years, American entrepreneurs led

the world in creating business organizations that set the pace for product development, production, and distribution. No wonder that these companies served as organizational models for businesses around the globe. American corporations delivered affordable factory-made goods, built and operated railroads that spanned the continent, created technological advances, such as the telephone and automobile, that changed the way we lived, and produced the highest standard of living the world had ever known. That these same companies and their descendants no longer perform well isn't because of some intrinsic flaw; it is because the world in which they operate has changed beyond the limits of their capacity to adjust or evolve. The principles on which they are organized were superbly suited to the conditions of an earlier era but can stretch only so far.

Advanced technologies, the disappearance of boundaries between national markets, and the altered expectations of customers who now have more choices than ever before have combined to make the goals, methods, and basic organizing principles of the classical American corporation sadly obsolete. Renewing their competitive capabilities isn't an issue of getting the people in these companies to work harder, but of learning to work differently. This means that companies and their employees must unlearn many of the principles and techniques that brought them success for so long.

Most companies today—no matter what business they are in, how technologically sophisticated their product or service, or what their national origin—can trace their work styles and organizational roots back to the prototypical pin factory that Adam Smith described in *The Wealth of Nations*, published in 1776. Smith, a philosopher and economist, recognized that the technology of the industrial revolution had created unprecedented opportunities for manufacturers to increase worker productivity and thus reduce the cost of goods, not by small percentages, which one might achieve by persuading an artisan to work a little faster, but by orders of magnitude. In *The Wealth of Nations*, this forebear of the business consultant, a radical thinker in his time, explained what he called the principle of the division of labor.

Smith's principle embodied his observations that some number of specialized workers, each performing a single step in the manufacture of a pin, could make far more pins in a day than the same number of generalists, each engaged in making whole pins. "One man," Smith wrote, "draws out the wire, another straightens it, a third cuts it, a fourth points it, a fifth grinds it at the top for receiving the head; to make the head requires two or three distinct operations; to put it on is a peculiar business, to whiten the pins is another; it is even a trade by itself to put them into the paper." Smith reported that he had visited a small factory, employing only ten people, each of whom was doing just one or two of the 18 specialized tasks involved in making a pin. "These ten persons could make among them upwards of forty-eight thousand pins in a day. But if they had all wrought separately and independently, and without any of them having been educated to this peculiar business, they certainly could not each of them have made twenty, perhaps not one pin in a day."

The division of labor increased the productivity of pin makers by a factor of hundreds. The advantage, Smith wrote, "is owing to three different circumstances; first, to the increase of dexterity in every particular workman; secondly, to the saving of the time which is commonly lost in passing from one species of work to another; and lastly, to the invention of a great number of machines which facilitate and abridge labor, and enable one man to do the work of many."

Today's airlines, steel mills, accounting firms, and computer chip makers have all been built around Smith's central idea—the division or specialization of labor and the consequent fragmentation of work. The larger the organization, the more specialized is the worker and the more separate steps into which the work is fragmented. This rule applies not only to manufacturing jobs. Insurance companies, for instance, typically assign separate clerks to process each line of a standardized form. They then pass the form to another clerk, who processes the next line. These workers never complete a job; they just perform piecemeal tasks.

Over time, American companies became the best in the world at translating Smith's organizing principles into working business organizations, even though, when Smith first published his ideas in 1776, not much of a domestic market existed for American-made goods. Americans, who numbered only 3.9 million, were separated from one another by bad roads and poor communications. Philadelphia, with 45,000 residents, was the fledgling nation's largest city.

Over the next half century, though, the population exploded and the domestic market expanded accordingly. The population of Philadelphia, for example, quadrupled, though New York was now the largest city with 313,000 people. Manufacturing facilities sprouted around the country.

Part of this growth occurred because of innovative changes in the ways in which goods could be shipped. In the 1820s, Americans began building railroads, which not only extended and accelerated economic development, but also moved the evolution of business management technology forward. It was railroad companies that invented the modern business bureaucracy—a significant innovation then and an essential one if industrial organizations were going to grow larger than the span of one person's control.

To prevent collisions on single-track lines that carried trains in both directions, railroad companies invented formalized operating procedures and the organizational structure and mechanisms required to carry them out. Management created a rule for every contingency they could imagine, and lines of authority and reporting were clearly drawn. The railroad companies literally programmed their workers to act only in accordance with the rules, which was the only way management knew to make their one-track systems predictable, workable, and safe. Programming people to conform to established procedures remains the essence of bureaucracy even now. The command-and-control systems in place in most companies today embody the same principles the railroads introduced a hundred and fifty years ago.

The next large evolutionary steps in the development of today's business organization came early in the twentieth century from two automobile pioneers: Henry Ford and Alfred Sloan.

Ford improved on Smith's concept of dividing work into tiny, repeatable tasks. Instead of having skilled assemblers build entire cars from parts they would fit together, Ford reduced each worker's job to installing a single part in a prescribed manner. Initially, workers walked from one assembly stand to the next, taking themselves to the work. The moving assembly line, the innovation for which Ford is best remembered, simply brought the work to the worker.

In breaking down car assembling into a series of uncomplicated tasks, Ford made the jobs themselves infinitely simpler, but he made the process of coordinating the people performing those jobs and of combining the results of their tasks into a whole car far more complex.

Then Alfred Sloan stepped in. Sloan, the successor to General Motors' founder William Durant, created the prototype of the management system that Ford's immensely more efficient factory system demanded.

Neither Henry Ford nor Durant ever learned how to manage the huge, sprawling organizations that their success with assembly-line production both necessitated and made possible—the engineering, manufacturing, assembly, and marketing operations. Durant, especially, with GM's far greater mix of cars and models, was constantly finding that the company had produced too many of one model for current market conditions or that production had to be suspended because not enough raw materials had been procured. After Sloan took over at GM, he made the system Ford had pioneered complete, and it is this total system to which the term mass production applies today.

Sloan created smaller, decentralized divisions that managers could oversee from a small corporate headquarters simply by monitoring production and financial numbers. Sloan set up one division for each car model—Chevrolet, Pontiac, Buick, Oldsmobile, and Cadillac—plus others making components such as generators (Delco) and steering gears (Saginaw).

Sloan was applying Adam Smith's principle of the division of labor to management just as Ford had applied it to production. In Sloan's view, corporate executives did not need specific expertise in engineering or manufacturing; specialists could oversee those functional areas. Instead, executives needed financial expertise. They had only to look at "the numbers"—sales, profit and loss, inventory levels, market share, and so forth—generated by the company's various divisions to see if those divisions were performing well; if not, they could demand appropriate corrective action.

Sloan's management innovations saved General Motors from early oblivion and, what's more, also solved the problems that had kept other companies from expanding. The new marketing specialists and financial managers that Sloan's system required complemented the company's engineering professionals. GM's head firmly established the division of professional labor in parallel with the division of manual labor that had already taken place on the factory floor.

The final evolutionary step in the development of corporations as we know them today came about in the United States between the end of World War II and the 1960s, a period of enormous economic expansion. The regimes of Robert McNamara at Ford, Harold Geneen at ITT, and Reginald Jones at General Electric epitomized management of that era. Through elaborate planning exercises, senior managers determined the businesses in which they wanted to be, how much capital they should allocate to each, and what returns they would expect the operating managers of these businesses to deliver to the company. Large staffs of corporate controllers, planners, and auditors acted as the executives' eyes and ears, ferreting out data about divisional performance, and intervening to adjust the plans and activities of operating managers.

The organizational model developed in the United States spread rapidly into Europe and then to Japan after World War II. Designed for a period of heavy and growing demand and therefore accelerating growth, this form of corporate organization suited the circumstances of the postwar times perfectly.

An unrelenting demand for goods and services, at home and abroad, shaped the economic environment of the time. Deprived of material goods, first by the Depression, then by the war, customers were more than happy to buy whatever companies offered them.

Rarely did they demand high quality and service. Any house, any car, any refrigerator were infinitely better than none at all.

In the 1950s and 1960s, the chief operational concern of company executives was capacity—that is, being able to keep up with ever-increasing demand. If a company built too much productive capacity too soon, it could go deep in the red financing its new plants. But if it built too little capacity or built it too late, the company could lose market share from its inability to produce. To solve these problems, companies developed ever more complex systems for budgeting, planning, and control.

The standard, pyramidal organizational structure of most organizations was well suited to a high-growth environment because it was scalable. When a company needed to grow, it could simply add workers as needed at the bottom of the chart and then fill in the management layers above.

This kind of organizational structure was also ideally suited for control and planning. By breaking work down into pieces, supervisors could ensure consistent and accurate worker performance, and the supervisors' supervisors could do the same. Budgets were easily approved and monitored department by department, and plans were generated and pursued on the same basis.

This organizational form also made for short training periods, since few production tasks were complicated or difficult. Moreover, as new office technology became available in the 1960s, companies were encouraged to break down even more of their white-collar work into small, repeatable tasks, which could also be mechanized or automated.

As the number of tasks grew, however, the overall processes of producing a product or delivering a service inevitably became increasingly complicated, and managing such process became more difficult. The growing number of people in the middle of the corporate organization chart—the functional or middle managers—was one of the prices companies paid for the benefits of fragmenting their work into simple, repetitive steps and organizing themselves hierarchically.

Another cost was the increasing distance that separated senior management from users of their product or service. Customers and their responses to the company's strategy became a set of faceless numbers that bubbled up through the layers.

These, then, are the roots of today's corporation, the principles, forged by necessity, on which today's companies have structured themselves. If modern companies thin slice work into meaningless tasks, it is because that is how efficiency was once achieved. If they diffuse power and responsibility through massive bureaucracies, it is because that was the way they learned to control sprawling enterprises. If they resist suggestions that they change the way they operate, it is because these organizing principles and the structures to which they gave birth have worked well for decades.

The reality that organizations have to confront, however, is that the old ways of doing business—the division of labor around which companies have been organized since Adam Smith first articulated the principle—simply don't work anymore. Suddenly, the world is a different place. The here-and-now crisis of competitiveness that American corporations face today is not the result of a temporary economic downturn or of a low point in the business cycle. Indeed, we can no longer even count on a predictable business cycle—prosperity, followed by recession, followed by renewed prosperity—as we once did. In today's environment, nothing is constant or predictable—not market growth, customer demand, product life cycles, the rate of technological change, or the nature of competition. Adam Smith's world and its way of doing business are yesterday's paradigm.

Three forces, separately and in combination, are driving today's companies deeper and deeper into territory that most of their executives and managers find frighteningly unfamiliar. We call these forces the three Cs: Customers, Competition, and Change. Their names are hardly new, but the characteristics of the three Cs are remarkably different from what they were in the past.

Let's look at the three Cs and how they have changed, beginning with customers.

• Customers take charge

Since the early 1980s, in the United States and other developed countries, the dominant force in the seller-customer relationship has shifted. Sellers no longer have the upper hand; customers do. Customers now tell suppliers what they want, when they want it, how they want it, and what they will pay. This new situation is unsettling to companies that have known life only in the mass market.

In reality, a mass market never existed, but for most of this century the *idea* of the mass market provided manufacturers and service providers—from Henry Ford's car company to Thomas Watson's computer company—with the useful fiction that their customers were more or less alike. If that were true, or if buyers behaved as if it were true, then companies could assume that a standard product or service—a black car or a big blue computer—would satisfy most of them. Even those that weren't satisfied would buy what was offered, because they had little choice. Mass market suppliers in the United States had relatively few competitors, most of which offered very similar products and services. In fact, most consumers weren't dissatisfied. They didn't know that anything better or different was available.

Now that they have choices, though, customers no longer behave as if they are all cast in the same mold. Customers— consumers and corporations alike—demand products and services designed for their unique and particular needs. There is no longer any such notion as *the* customer; there is only *this* customer, the one with whom a seller is dealing at the moment and who now has the capacity to indulge his or her own personal tastes. The mass market has broken into pieces, some as small as a single customer.

Individual customers—whether consumers or industrial firms— demand that they be treated individually. They expect products that are configured to their needs, delivery schedules that match their manufacturing plans or work hours, and payment terms that are convenient for them. Individually and in combination, a number of factors have contributed to shifting the balance of market power from producer to consumer.

Consumer expectations soared in the United States when competitors—many of them Japanese—burst upon the market with lower prices combined with higher quality goods. Then the Japanese introduced new products that established American producers had not had time to bring to market—or maybe hadn't even thought of yet. What's more, the Japanese did it all with levels of service that traditional companies could not match. This was mass production *plus*—plus quality, price, selection, and service.

In the service sector, consumers expect and demand more, because they know they can *get* more. Technology, in the form of sophisticated, easily accessible databases, allows service providers and retailers of all kinds to track not only basic information about their customers, but their preferences and requirements, thereby laying a new foundation for competitiveness.

In Houston, if a customer calls Pizza Hut to order a pepperoni and mushroom pie, the same kind of pizza that the customer ordered last week, the clerk asks if the caller would like to try a new combination. If the person says "yes," the clerk mails him or her discount coupons with offerings customized to that individual's tastes. When a consumer calls Whirlpool's service line, the call is automatically routed to the same service representative with whom the consumer spoke last time, creating a sense of personal relationship and intimacy in a world of 800 numbers. Mail-order retailers, which have the capability of collecting enormous amounts of data about their customers, have perfected an even higher targeted level of service. Once customers experience this superior service, they do not happily return to accepting less.

The incredible consolidation of customers in some markets—the growth of megadealers in the automobile business, the handful of fast-food franchises replacing thousands of independent eateries, and the mall-sized discounters that have emptied Main Street store fronts—has also profoundly changed the terms of the seller-customer relationship. If the sign out front now reads "Joe Smith's Oldsmobile, Nissan, Isuzu, Mercedes, Jeep, Honda, and Saturn," then Joe Smith, not General Motors, has the upper hand in their negotiations. With so many other brands available to him, Joe needs General Motors less than GM needs him.

The threat of backward integration has also helped to shift power from producers to consumers. Often, customers now can do for themselves what suppliers used to do for them. Companies may not want to, but they can buy the same machines and hire the same people as their vendors. "Do it my way," they can say, "or I will do it myself." Inexpensive and easy-to-learn desktop publishing technology, for instance, gives companies the choice of doing for themselves jobs for which they used to rely on printers.

What holds true for industrial customers also holds true for consumers. When individual depositors realized that they could themselves purchase the same high-grade, short-term government securities and commercial paper that the banks were buying with their deposit money, many of them reduced their balances in those low interest-bearing accounts, depriving the banks of an important source of revenue.

Customers have gained the upper hand in their relationships with sellers, in part, because customers now have easy access to enormously more data. The information-rich world made possible by new communications technologies doesn't even require the consumer to have a computer at home. Anyone can, for instance, pick up a daily newspaper and compare rates on CDs from banks all around the country. Publishers collect that data electronically and pass it on to readers, who now know positively if their local bank is offering a good deal and if not, who is. An auto dealer today has to assume that any customer has read the appropriate issue of *Consumer Reports* and is well aware of what the dealer paid the manufacturer for the car. This makes the negotiation process decidedly trickier for the dealer.

For companies that grew up with a mass market mentality, the hardest new reality to accept about customers is that *each one counts*. Lose a customer today and another doesn't just appear. For thirty years after World War II, consumer goods were in chronically short supply. Manufacturers could not produce enough of them at prices sufficiently low to satisfy every possible buyer. The effect of insatiable demand was to give producers the advantage over buyers. In a mass market, to paraphrase the movie, *Field of Dreams*, if you build it they will buy.

Consumer goods shortages no longer exist. On the supply side of the equation, more producers now operate around the world. On the demand side, developed countries now have lower population growths. Also, many product markets have matured. Almost everyone who wants one now owns a refrigerator, a videocassette recorder, and even a personal computer. Those industries are in a replacement mode. Consequently, consumers wield a great deal of power. They can, in other words, be very choosy.

In short, in place of the expanding mass markets of the 1950s, 1960s, and 1970s, companies today have customers—business customers and individual consumers—who know what they want, what they want to pay for it, and how to get it on the terms they demand. Customers such as these don't need to deal with companies that don't understand and appreciate this startling change in the customer-buyer relationship.

• Competition intensifies

The second C is competition. It used to be so simple: The company that could get to market with an acceptable product or service at the best price would get a sale. Now, not only does more competition exist, it's of many different kinds.

Niche competitors have changed the face of practically every market. Similar goods sell in different markets on entirely disparate competitive bases: in one market on the basis of price, in another on selection, somewhere else on quality, and elsewhere on service before, during, or after the sale. With trade barriers falling, no company's national turf is protected from overseas competition. When the Japanese—or Germans, French, Koreans, Taiwanese, and so forth—are free to compete in the same markets, just one superior performer can raise the competitive threshold for companies around the world. Caterpillar competes with Komatsu, DuPont with Hoechst, Chase Manhattan with Barclays. Good performers drive out the inferior, because the lowest price, the highest quality, the best service available from any one of them soon becomes the standard for all competitors. Adequate is no longer good enough. If a company can't stand shoulder to shoulder with the world's best in a competitive category, it soon has no place to stand at all.

Start-up companies that carry no organizational baggage and are not constrained by their histories can enter a market with the next product or service generation before existing companies can even recoup their development costs on the last one. Big is no longer impregnable, and every established company today needs to post a lookout for start-ups—those that are brand new and those that have been around for a while but still operate on their founders' principles. By that definition, Sun Microsystems is still a start-up, and so is Wal-Mart. Sun's workstation innovation changed the course of history for every computer maker in the world. Wal-Mart reinvented retailing.

Start-ups do not play by the rules. They write new rules about how to run a business. Wal-Mart did not create itself in the image of Sears. Unburdened by Sears's past, it conceived new ways of working that produce better results. Sears's apparent assets—lots of stores employing well-trained salespeople, established supplier relationships, smoothly tuned operating and administrative systems—have turned into liabilities in that they cannot produce the results that Wal-Mart has established as the new competitive standards.

Technology changes the nature of competition in ways companies don't expect. In retailing, for instance, it has allowed manufacturers and retailers, such as Procter & Gamble and Wal-Mart, to merge their distribution and inventory systems in ways that are mutually beneficial. In after-sales service, technology allows innovators to devise entirely new service techniques. Otis Elevator Company, for example, has developed an ingenious computer system for managing the Byzantine task of servicing ninety-three thousand elevators and escalators in North America around the clock. Repair technicians arrive at the scene already briefed on the nature of the problem and the particular machine's maintenance history. By innovating with technology in order to streamline the interaction between themselves and their customers, companies such as Otis expand the limits of the possible, thereby raising customer expectations for all the companies in a market.

• Change becomes constant

Change is the third C. We already know that customers and competition have changed, but so, too, has the nature of change itself. Foremost, change has become both pervasive and persistent. It *is* normality.

Not long ago, for example, life insurance companies offered only two products: term and whole life. Today, they supply a constantly changing smorgasbord of products, and the competitive pressure on insurance companies to create new products is constantly increasing.

Moreover, the pace of change has accelerated. With globalization of the economy, companies face a greater number of competitors, each one of which may introduce product and service innovations to the market. The rapidity of technological change also promotes innovation. Product life cycles have gone from years to months. Ford produced the Model T for an entire human generation. The life cycle of a computer product introduced today might stretch to two years, but probably won't. A company in the pension business recently developed a service to take advantage of a quirk in the tax laws and interest rates. Its anticipated market life was exactly three months. Coming to this market late by just thirty days would have cut the company's selling time for the service by a third.

The point is that not only have product and service life cycles diminished, but so has the time available to develop new products and introduce them. Today, companies must move fast, or they won't be moving at all.

Moreover, they have to be looking in many directions at once. Executives *think* their companies are equipped with effective change-sensing radars, but most of them aren't. Mostly what they detect are the changes they expect. The brand managers at a consumer goods manufacturer we know assiduously tracked consumer attitudes in order to detect shifts that might affect their products. Their surveys kept giving them good news, but market share took a sudden drop. They did more surveys. Customers loved the products, but market share kept tumbling. It turned out the problem was that the company's sloppy order fulfillment process was infuriating its retailers, who responded by cutting its shelf space, but neither the brand managers nor anyone else at the company had a broad enough perspective to detect and deal with this problem.

The changes that will put a company out of business are those that happen outside the light of its current expectations, and that is the source of most change in today's business environment.

The three Cs—customers, competition, and change—have created a new world for business, and it is becoming increasingly apparent that organizations designed to operate in one environment cannot be fixed to work well in another. Companies created to thrive on mass production, stability, and growth can't be fixed to succeed in a world where customers, competition, and change demand flexibility and quick response.

Some people blame corporate America's problems on factors beyond managements' control—closed foreign markets, the low cost of Japanese capital, and predatory pricing by foreign companies subsidized by their governments. They blame the federal government's mishandling of the economy, its regulations, and its poor husbandry of natural and human resources. They blame unions or poorly educated and unmotivated American workers.

But if these reasons accounted for our dilemma, nearly all American companies would be in decline. But they aren't. Sears may be losing its market, but Wal-Mart and The Gap are thriving. GM has trouble making world-class cars in America, but Honda doesn't. The insurance industry, as a whole, may be hemorrhaging money, but some companies, such as Progressive Insurance, earn outstanding returns. Bethlehem Steel has shrunk to a tenth of its former size, but Nucor and other minimills perform well in the global market. In almost every industry, under the same rules and with the same players, the successes of a few companies rebut the excuses of the many.

If American managers can't decide why their companies are in trouble, neither do they agree on what to do about it. Some people think American companies would bounce back if only they had the right products and services for the times. We reject that thinking, because products have limited lifespans, and even the best soon become obsolete. It is not products but the processes that create products that bring companies long-term success. Good products don't make winners; winners make good products.

Some people think companies could cure what ails them by changing their corporate strategies. They should sell one division and buy another, change their markets, get into a different business. They should juggle assets or restructure with a leveraged buyout (LBO). But this kind of thinking distracts companies from making basic changes in the real work they actually do. It also bespeaks a profound contempt for the daily operations of business. Companies are not asset portfolios, but people working together to invent, make, sell, and provide service. If they are not succeeding in the businesses that they are in, it is because their people are not inventing, making, selling, and servicing as well as they should. Playing tycoon might be more exciting for senior managers than dirtying their hands in the mundane details of operations, but it is not more important. "God," said the architect Mies van der Rohe, "is in the details." Van der Rohe was speaking of buildings, but his observation applies equally well to running a business.

Some people, including many managers, blame corporate problems on management deficiencies. If companies were only managed differently and better, they would thrive. But none of the management fads of the last twenty years—not management by objectives, diversification, Theory Z, zero-based budgeting, value chain analysis, decentralization, quality circles, "excellence," restructuring, portfolio management, management by walking around, matrix management, intrapreneuring, or one-minute managing—has reversed the deterioration of America's corporate competitive performance. They have only distracted managers from the real task at hand.

Some people think that automation is the answer to business problems. True, computers can speed work up, and in the past forty years businesses have spent billions of dollars to automate tasks that people once did by hand. Automating does get some jobs done faster. But fundamentally the same jobs are being done, and that means no fundamental improvements in performance.

Our diagnosis of America's business problems is simple, but the corrective action that it demands is not as easy to implement as the solutions that have already been tried. Our diagnosis goes to the very heart of what a company does. It rests on the premise that a company that is better than others at the meat and potatoes of its business—inventing products and services, manufacturing or providing them, selling them, filling orders, and serving customers—will beat the competition in the marketplace. We believe that, in general, the difference between winning companies and losers is that winning companies know how to do their work better. If American companies want to become winners again, they will have to look to how they get their work done. It is as simple and as formidable as that.

To illustrate what we mean when we talk about a company getting its work done, let's look at a common process found in practically every company in America. Order fulfillment begins when a customer places an order, ends when the goods are delivered, and includes everything in between. Typically, the process involves a dozen or so steps performed by different people in different departments. Someone in customer service receives the order, logs it in, and checks it for completeness and accuracy. Then the order goes to finance, where someone else runs a credit check on the customer. Next, someone in sales operations determines the price to charge. Then the order travels to inventory control, where someone checks to see if the goods are on hand. If not, the order gets routed to production planning, which issues a back order. Eventually, warehouse operations develops a shipment schedule. Traffic determines the shipment method—rail, truck, air, or water—and picks the route and carrier. Product handling picks the products from the warehouse, verifies the accuracy of the order, assembles the pickings, and loads them. Traffic releases the goods to the carrier, which takes responsibility for delivering them to the customer.

This process may be complex, but, when viewed from the perspective of Adam Smith's division of labor principle and Alfred Sloan's principles of management control and accountability, it does have certain advantages. First, companies don't have to hire people with advanced degrees to get it done. Every person involved in the process has specific responsibility for performing one simple task. Second, everyone in the process is accountable through the bureaucratic chain of command.

Companies must accept trade-offs, however, for keeping the tasks simple and maintaining tight control of employee actions. First, because no one in the company oversees the whole process and its result, no *one* person is responsible for it. No one involved in the process can tell a customer where the order is and when it will arrive. Many people are involved in order fulfillment, but it is no single person's job or the job of any *one* functional unit.

Second, the process is error prone. Errors are inevitable with so many people having to handle and act separately on the same order.

Preaching quality won't help. Even if every person involved in order fulfillment did his or her job perfectly and in exactly the time allotted, the process would still be slow and error prone. Too many handoffs exist—nine at least, and more if the order is placed on back order. Each handoff entails queues, batches, and wait times.

Furthermore, classical order fulfillment involves no element of customer service at all. Complex processes involving a dozen people working across departmental lines can't be made flexible enough to deal with special requests or to respond to inquiries. No one is empowered to answer a question or solve a problem. Once an order enters the process, it might as well be lost until it emerges at the other end—whenever that might turn out to be.

Merely fixing the pieces of the order fulfillment process won't solve the larger problem. Companies that try to improve their performance by working on the pieces of the process miss this point. In fact, trying to fix what's wrong with American companies by tinkering with the individual process pieces is the best way we know to *guarantee* continued bad business performance. Yet, in company after company we have seen, management works at fixing the pieces instead of redesigning the processes by which the company's work gets done.

The core message of our book, then, is this: It is no longer necessary or desirable for companies to organize their work around Adam Smith's division of labor. Task-oriented jobs in today's world of customers, competition, and change are obsolete. Instead, companies must organize work around *process*.

This is an assertion as radical and as far-reaching today as Adam Smith's was in his time. Managers who understand and accept this concept of process-based work will help their companies leap ahead. Those who don't will stay behind.

We write about "processes" throughout the rest of this book, but already it should be apparent why a process perspective is so important to any company that would find its way out of the dilemma that currently confounds American business. It should already be possible to see why American companies can't be fixed but have to be reinvented.

In most companies today, no one is in charge of the processes. In fact, hardly anyone is even aware of them. Does any company have a vice president in charge of order fulfillment, of getting products to customers? Probably not. Who is in *charge* of developing new products? Everyone—R&D, marketing, finance, manufacturing, and so on—is involved, but no one is in charge.

Companies today consist of functional silos, or stovepipes, vertical structures built on narrow pieces of a process. The person checking the customer's credit is part of the credit department, which is probably part of the finance organization. Inventory picking is performed by workers in the warehouse, who may report to the vice president of manufacturing. Shipping, on the other hand, is part of logistics. People involved in a process look *inward* toward their department and *upward* toward their boss, but no one looks *outward* toward the customer. The contemporary performance problems that companies experience are the inevitable consequences of process fragmentation.

Classical business structures that specialize work and fragment processes are self-perpetuating because they stifle innovation and creativity in an organization. If someone in a functional department actually has a new idea—a better way of filling customer orders, for instance—he or she first has to sell it to the boss, who has to sell it to his or her boss, and so on up the corporate hierarchy. For an idea to win acceptance, everyone along the way must say yes, but killing an idea requires only one no. From the point of view of its designers, this built-in innovation damper is not a flaw in the classic structure but a safeguard against change that might introduce unwarranted risk.

The fragmented processes and specialized structures of companies bred for an earlier day also are unresponsive to large changes in the external environment—the market. Existing process design embodies the assumption that conditions will vary only within narrow, predictable limits. By removing management from operations and fracturing those operations among specialized departments, today's organizations ensure that no one will be in a position to recognize significant change or, if he or she should happen to recognize it, to do anything about it.

Today, fragmented organizations display appalling diseconomies of scale, quite the opposite of what Adam Smith envisioned. The diseconomies show up not in direct labor, but in overhead. If, for instance, an organization does 100 units of work an hour, and each of its workers can do 10 units an hour, the company would need 11 people: 10 workers and 1 supervisor. But if demand for the company's output grew tenfold to 1,000 units of work an hour, the company wouldn't need just 10 times the number of workers plus one manager for each 10 new workers. It would need something like 196 people: 100 workers, 10 supervisors, 1 manager, 3 assistant managers, 18 people in a human resources organization, 19 people in long-range planning, 22 in audit and control, and 23 in facilitation and expediting.

This diseconomy of scale is not just bureaucratic proliferation and empire-building, although some of that may be at work too. Rather, it is a consequence of what we call the Humpty Dumpty School of Organizational Management. Companies take a natural process, such as order fulfillment, and break it into lots of little pieces—the individual tasks that people in the functional departments do. Then, the company has to hire all the king's horses and all the king's men to paste the fragmented work back together again. These king's horses and king's men have titles such as auditor, expediter, controller, liaison, supervisor, manager, and vice president. They are simply the glue that holds together the people who do the real work—the credit checkers, the inventory pickers, the package shippers. In many companies, direct labor costs may be down, but overhead costs are up—way up. Most companies today, in other words, are paying more for the glue than for the real work—a recipe for trouble.

Inflexibility, unresponsiveness, the absence of customer focus, an obsession with activity rather than result, bureaucratic paralysis, lack of innovation, high overhead—these are the legacies of one hundred years of American industrial leadership. These characteristics are not new; they have not suddenly appeared. They have been present all along. It is just that until recently, American companies didn't have to worry much about them. If costs were high, they could be passed on to customers. If customers were dissatisfied, they had nowhere else to turn. If new products were slow in coming, customers would wait. The important managerial job was to manage growth, and the rest didn't matter. Now that growth has flattened out, the rest matters a great deal.

America's business problem is that it is entering the twenty-first century with companies designed during the nineteenth century to work well in the twentieth.

We need something entirely different.

CHAPTER 2

REENGINEERING—THE PATH TO CHANGE

When someone asks us for a quick definition of business reengineering, we say that it means "starting over." It *doesn't* mean tinkering with what already exists or making incremental changes that leave basic structures intact. It isn't about making patchwork fixes—jury-rigging existing systems so that they work better. It does mean abandoning long-established procedures and looking afresh at the work required to create a company's product or service and deliver value to the customer. It means asking this question: "If I were re-creating this company today, given what I know and given current technology, what would it look like?" Reengineering a company means tossing aside old systems and starting over. It involves going back to the beginning and inventing a better way of doing work.

This informal definition is fine for conversation, because it gives people an idea of what we mean by business reengineering. But anyone who wants to apply reengineering to a company needs something more.

How does a company reengineer its business processes? Where does it begin? Who gets involved? Where do the ideas for radical change come from?

We have watched companies use trial and error to answer these questions about radical change. We have served as advisers to companies that have made such changes and have observed others. Out of their experiences and our own emerged the concept of business reengineering, which we have developed into a process for reinventing a company. To perform this process, we and the companies with which we have worked have developed a body of techniques. These are not formulas, but tools that companies can use to reinvent the way their work gets done.

Our experiences and those of our clients with these techniques are encouraging. Used properly—that is, with intelligence and imagination—they work and can lead to breathtaking improvements in performance. The balance of this book is about business reengineering and how people can make it succeed in their companies.

REENGINEERING FORMALLY DEFINED

Let's begin, then, with a better definition. "Reengineering," properly, is "the fundamental rethinking and radical redesign of business processes to achieve dramatic improvements in critical, contemporary measures of performance, such as cost, quality, service, and speed." This definition contains four key words.

KEY WORD: FUNDAMENTAL

The first key word is "fundamental." In doing reengineering, businesspeople must ask the most basic questions about their companies and how they operate: *Why* do we do what we do? And why do we do it the way we do? Asking these fundamental questions forces people to look at the tacit rules and assumptions that underlie the way they conduct their businesses. Often, these rules turn out to be obsolete, erroneous, or inappropriate.

Reengineering begins with no assumptions and no givens; in fact, companies that undertake reengineering must guard against the assumptions that most processes already have embedded in them. To ask "How can we perform customer credit checks more efficiently?" assumes that customer credit must be checked. In many instances, the cost of checking may, in fact, exceed the bad-debt losses that checking avoids. Reengineering first determines *what* a company must do, then *how* to do it. Reengineering takes nothing for granted. It ignores what *is* and concentrates on what *should be*.

KEY WORD: RADICAL

The second key word in our definition is radical, which is derived from the Latin word "radix," meaning root. Radical redesign means getting to the root of things: not making superficial changes or fiddling with what is already in place, but throwing away the old. In reengineering, radical redesign means disregarding all existing structures and procedures and inventing completely new ways of accomplishing work. Reengineering is about business *reinvention*—not business improvement, business enhancement, or business modification.

KEY WORD: DRAMATIC

The third key word is *dramatic*. Reengineering isn't about making marginal or incremental improvements but about achieving quantum leaps in performance. If a company falls 10 percent short of where it should be, if its costs come in 10 percent too high, if its quality is 10 percent too low, if its customer service performance needs a 10-percent boost, that company does *not* need reengineering. More conventional methods, from exhorting the troops to establishing incremental quality programs, can dig a company out of a 10-percent hole. Reengineering should be brought in only when a need exists for heavy blasting. Marginal improvement requires fine-tuning; dramatic improvement demands blowing up the old and replacing it with something new.

From our experience, we have identified three kinds of companies that undertake reengineering. First are companies that find themselves in deep trouble. They have no choice. If a company's costs are an order of magnitude higher than the competition's or than its business model will allow, if its customer service is so abysmal that customers openly rail against it, if its product failure rate is twice, three times, or five times as great as the competition's, if, in other words, it needs order-of-magnitude improvement, that company clearly needs business reengineering. Ford Motor Company in the early 1980s is a case in point.

Second are companies that are not yet in trouble but whose management has the foresight to see trouble coming. Aetna Life & Casualty in the last half of the 1980s is an example. For the time being, financial results may appear satisfactory, but looming in the distance are storm clouds—new competitors, changing customer requirements or characteristics, an altered regulatory or economic environment—that threaten to sweep away the foundations of the company's success. These companies have the vision to begin reengineering in advance of running into adversity.

The third type of company undertaking reengineering are those that are in peak condition. They have no discernible difficulties, either now or on the horizon, but their managements are ambitious and aggressive. Examples include Hallmark and Wal-Mart. Companies in this third category see reengineering as an opportunity to further their lead over their competitors. By enhancing their performance, they seek to raise the competitive bar even higher and make life even tougher for everyone else. Clearly, reengineering from a position of strength is hard to do. Why rewrite the rules when you're already winning the game? It has been said that the hallmark of the truly successful company is a willingness to abandon what has long been successful. A truly great company is never satisfied with its current performance. A truly great company willingly abandons practices that have long worked well in the hope and expectation of coming up with something better.

We sometimes explain the distinctions among these three kinds of companies this way: Companies in the first category are desperate; they have hit the wall and are lying injured on the ground. Companies in the second category are cruising along at high speed, but see something rushing toward them in their head lamps. Could it be a wall? Companies in the third category are out for a drive on a clear afternoon, with no obstacles in sight. What a splendid time, they decide, to stop and build a wall for the other guys.

KEY WORD: PROCESSES

The fourth key word in our definition is *processes*. Although this word is the most important in our definition, it is also the one that gives most corporate managers the greatest difficulty. Most businesspeople are not "process-oriented"; they are focused on tasks, on jobs, on people, on structures, but not on processes.

We define a business process as a collection of activities that takes one or more kinds of input and creates an output that is of value to the customer. We illustrated a process in Chapter 1 when we talked about order fulfillment, which takes an order as its input and results in the delivery of the ordered goods. In other words, the delivery of the ordered goods to the customer's hands is the value that the process creates.

Under the influence of Adam Smith's notion of breaking work into its simplest tasks and assigning each of these to a specialist, modern companies and their managers focus on the individual tasks in this process—receiving the order form, picking the goods from the warehouse, and so forth—and tend to lose sight of the larger objective, which is to get the goods into the hands of the customer who ordered them. The individual tasks within this process are important, but none of them matters one whit to the customer if the overall process doesn't work—that is, if the process doesn't deliver the goods.

We will use three examples of reengineering to illustrate how it works and what it can accomplish for companies. In reading these examples, it is helpful to keep in mind the four key words that characterize reengineering—fundamental, radical, dramatic, and process—but especially process. Task-based thinking—the fragmentation of work into its simplest components and their assignment to specialist workers—has influenced the organizational design of companies for the last two hundred years. The shift to process-based thinking is already underway, and that shift is illustrated in the radical changes that mainstream companies such as IBM Credit, Ford Motor, and Kodak have made.

Example: IBM Credit

Our first case concerns IBM Credit Corporation, a wholly owned subsidiary of IBM, which, if it were independent, would rank among the *Fortune* 100 service companies. IBM Credit is in the business of financing the computers, software, and services that the IBM Corporation sells. It is a business of which IBM is fond, since financing customers' purchases is an extremely profitable business.

In its early years, IBM Credit's operation was positively Dickensian. When an IBM field salesperson called in with a request for financing, he or she reached one of fourteen people sitting around a conference room table in Old Greenwich, Connecticut. The person taking the call logged the request for a deal on a piece of paper. That was step one.

In step two, someone carted that piece of paper upstairs to the credit department, where a specialist entered the information into a computer system and checked the potential borrower's creditworthiness. The specialist wrote the results of the credit check on the piece of paper and dispatched it to the next link in the chain, which was the business practices department.

The business practices department, step three, was in charge of modifying the standard loan covenant in response to customer request. Business practices had its own computer system. When done, a person in that department would attach the special terms to the request form.

Next, the request went to a pricer, step four, who keyed the data into a personal computer spreadsheet to determine the appropriate interest rate to charge the customer. The pricer wrote the rate on a piece of paper, which, with the other papers, was delivered to a clerical group, step five.

There, an administrator turned all this information into a quote letter that could be delivered to the field sales representative by Federal Express.

The entire process consumed six days on average, although it sometimes took as long as two weeks. From the sales reps' point of view, this turnaround was too long, since it gave the customer six days to find another source of financing, to be seduced by another computer vendor, or simply to call the whole deal off. So the rep would call—and call and call—to ask, "Where is my deal, and when are you going to get it out?" Naturally, no one had a clue, since the request was lost somewhere in the chain.

In their efforts to improve this process, IBM Credit tried several fixes. They decided, for instance, to install a control desk, so they could answer the rep's questions about the status of the deal. That is, instead of each department forwarding the credit request to the next step in the chain, it would return it to the control desk where the calls were originally taken. There, an administrator logged the completion of each step before sending the paper out again. This fix did indeed solve one problem: The control desk knew the location of each request in the labyrinth and could give the rep the information he or she wanted. Unfortunately, this information was purchased at the cost of adding more time to the turnaround.

Eventually, two senior managers at IBM Credit had a brainstorm. They took a financing request and walked it themselves through all five steps, asking personnel in each office to put aside whatever they were doing and to process this request as they normally would, only without the delay of having it sit in a pile on someone's desk. They learned from their experiments that performing the actual work took in total only *ninety minutes*—one and one half hours. The remainder—now more than seven days on the average—was consumed by handing the form off from one department to the next. Management had begun to look at the heart of the issue, which was the overall credit issuance process. Indeed, if by the wave of some magic wand the company were able to double the personal productivity of each individual in the organization, total turnaround time would have been reduced by only forty-five minutes. The problem did not lie in the tasks and the people performing them, but in the structure of the process itself. In other words, it was the process that had to change, not the individual steps.

In the end, IBM Credit replaced its specialists—the credit checkers, pricers, and so on—with generalists. Now, instead of sending an application from office to office, one person called a deal structurer processes the entire application from beginning to end: No handoffs.

How could one generalist replace four specialists? The old process design was, in fact, founded on a deeply held (but deeply hidden) assumption: that every bid request was unique and difficult to process, thereby requiring the intervention of four highly trained specialists. In fact, this assumption was false; most requests were simple and straightforward. The old process had been overdesigned to handle the most difficult applications that management could imagine. When IBM Credit's senior managers closely examined the work the specialists did, they found that most of it was little more than clerical: finding a credit rating in a database, plugging numbers into a standard model, pulling boilerplate clauses from a file. These tasks fall well within the capability of a single individual when he or she is supported by an easy-to-use computer system that provides access to all the data and tools the specialists would use.

IBM Credit also developed a new, sophisticated computer system to support the deal structurers. In most situations, the system provides the deal structurer with the guidance needed to proceed. In really tough situations, he or she can get help from a small pool of real specialists—experts in credit checking, pricing, and so forth. Even here handoffs have disappeared because the deal structurer and the specialists he or she calls in work together as a team.

The performance improvement achieved by the redesign is extraordinary. IBM Credit slashed its seven-*day* turnaround to four *hours*. It did so *without* an increase in head count—in fact, it has achieved a small head-count reduction. At the same time, the number of deals that it handles has increased a hundredfold. Not 100 percent, but *one hundred times*.

What IBM Credit accomplished—a 90-percent reduction in cycle time and a hundredfold improvement in productivity—easily meets our definition of reengineering. The company achieved a *dramatic* performance breakthrough by making a *radical* change to the *process* as a whole. IBM Credit did not ask, "How do we improve the calculation of a financing quote? How do we enhance credit checking?" It asked instead, "How do we improve the credit issuance process?" Furthermore, in making its radical change, IBM Credit shattered the assumption that it needed specialists to perform specialized steps.

Example: Ford Motor

Our second example of reengineering involves changes to a different category of process. We defined a process as a series of activities that delivers value to a customer and cited order fulfillment and credit issuance as examples. However, the customer of a process is not necessarily a customer of the company. The customer may be inside the company, as it is, for instance, for the materials acquisition or purchasing process, which supplies materials to a company's manufacturing operations. Reengineering can apply to these processes, too, as Ford Motor Company learned.

In the early 1980s, Ford, like many other American corporations, was searching for ways to cut overhead and administrative costs. One of the places Ford believed it could reduce costs was in its accounts payable department, the organization that paid the bills submitted by Ford's suppliers. At that time, Ford's North American accounts payable department employed more than five hundred people. By using computers to automate some functions, Ford executives believed that they could attain a 20 percent head-count reduction in the department, bringing the number of clerks down to four hundred. By our definition, this incremental improvement, achieved by automating the existing manual process, would not qualify as business reengineering. Nonetheless, Ford managers thought 20 percent sounded pretty good—until they visited Mazda.

Ford had recently acquired a 25 percent equity interest in the Japanese company. The Ford executives noted that the admittedly smaller company took care of its accounts payable chores with only *five* people. The contrast—Ford's five hundred people to Mazda's five—was too great to attribute just to the smaller company's size, *esprit de corps*, company songs, or morning calisthenics. Automating to achieve a 20 percent personnel reduction clearly would not put Ford on a cost-par with Mazda, so the Ford executives were forced to rethink the entire process in which the accounts payable department took part.

This decision marked a critical shift in perspective for Ford, because companies can reengineer only business processes, not the administrative organizations that have evolved to accomplish them. "Accounts payable" cannot be reengineered, because it is not a process. It is a department, an organizational artifact of a particular process design. The accounts payable department consists of a group of clerks sitting in a room and passing paper amongst themselves. *They* cannot be reengineered, but what they *do* can be—and the way they are eventually reorganized to accomplish the new work process will follow from the requirements of the reengineered process itself.

We cannot emphasize this crucial distinction enough. Reengineering must focus on redesigning a fundamental business process, not on departments or other organizational units. Define a reengineering effort in terms of an organizational unit, and the effort is doomed. Once a real work process is reengineered, the shape of the organizational structure required to perform the work will become apparent. It probably will not look much like the old organization; some departments or other organizational units may even disappear, as they did at Ford.

The process that Ford eventually reengineered was not "accounts payable," but "procurement." That process took as input a purchase order from, say, a plant that needed parts and provided that plant (the process customer) with bought-and-paid-for goods. The procurement process included the accounts payable function, but it also encompassed purchasing and receiving.

Ford's old parts acquisition process was remarkably conventional. It began with the purchasing department sending a purchase order to a vendor, with a copy going to accounts payable. When the vendor shipped the goods and they arrived at Ford, a clerk at the receiving dock would complete a form describing the goods and send it to accounts payable. The vendor, meanwhile, sent accounts payable an invoice.

Accounts payable now had three documents relating to these goods—the purchase order, the receiving document, and the invoice. If all three matched, a clerk issued payment. Most of the time, that is what happened, but occasionally Vilfredo Pareto intervened.

Pareto, an early twentieth-century Italian economist, formulated what most of us call the 80-20 rule, technically known as the law of maldistribution. This rule states that 80 percent of the effort expended in a process is caused by only 20 percent of the input. In the case of Ford's accounts payable department, clerks there spent the great majority of their time straightening out the infrequent situations in which the documents—purchase order, receiving document, and invoice—did not match. Sometimes, the resolution required weeks of time and enormous amounts of work in order to trace and clarify the discrepancies.

Ford's new accounts payable process looks radically different. Accounts payable clerks no longer match purchase order with invoice with receiving document, primarily because the new process eliminates the invoice entirely. The results have proved dramatic. Instead of five hundred people, Ford now has just 125 people involved in vendor payment.

The new process looks like this: When a buyer in the purchasing department issues a purchase order to a vendor, that buyer simultaneously enters the order into an on-line database. Vendors, as before, send goods to the receiving dock. When they arrive, someone in receiving checks a computer terminal to see whether the received shipment corresponds to an outstanding purchase order in the database. Only two possibilities exist: It does or it doesn't. If it does, the clerk at the dock accepts the goods and pushes a button on the terminal keyboard that tells the database that the goods have arrived. Receipt of the goods is now recorded in the database, and the computer will automatically issue and send a check to the vendor at the appropriate time. If, on the other hand, the goods do not correspond to an outstanding purchase order in the database, the clerk on the dock will refuse the shipment and send it back to the vendor.

The basic concept of the change at Ford is simple. Payment authorization, which used to be performed by accounts payable, is now accomplished at the receiving dock. The old process fostered Byzantine complexities: searches, suspense files, ticklers—enough to keep five hundred clerks more or less busy. The new process does not. In fact, the new process comes close to eliminating the need for an accounts payable department altogether. In some parts of Ford, such as the Engine Division, the head count in accounts payable is now just 5 percent of its former size. Only a handful of people remains to handle exceptional situations.

The reengineered process at Ford breaks hard and fast rules that formerly applied there. Every business has these rules, deeply ingrained in the operation of the organization, whether they are explicitly spelled out or not.

For instance, Rule One at Ford's accounts payable department was: We pay when we receive the invoice. While this rule was rarely articulated, it was the frame around which the old process was formed. When Ford's managers reinvented this process, they were effectively asking whether they still wanted to live by this rule. The answer was no. The way to break this rule was to eliminate invoices. Instead of "We pay when we receive the *invoice*," the new rule at Ford is, "We pay when we receive the *goods*." Altering just that one word established the basis for a major business change. Other one-word changes in old rules at Ford are having similar effects today.

In one of its truck plants, for instance, instead of "We pay when we receive the goods," Ford has implemented an even newer rule: "We pay when we *use* the goods." The company has said in effect to one of its brake suppliers, "We like your brakes, and we will continue to install them on our trucks, but until we do, they are *your* brakes, not ours. The brakes only become ours when we use them, and that's when we'll pay for them. Every time a truck comes off the line with a set of your brakes on it, we'll mail you a check." This change has simplified even further Ford's purchasing and receiving procedures. (It also has paid off in other ways, from reducing inventory levels to improving cash flow.)

The new process for brake acquisition shatters another rule at Ford, the one that requires the company always to maintain multiple sources of supply. At least with regard to truck brakes, the new rule is, "We shall have a *single* source of supply and work *very* closely with that vendor."

One might wonder why the brake supplier agreed to this change, since it is now, for practical purposes, financing Ford's brake inventory. What benefit does the supplier derive from the new arrangement?

First, it now gets all of Ford's truck brake business instead of just some of it. Second, because the supplier is now privy to Ford's computerized manufacturing schedule, it does not have to depend on the unreliable forecasts of Ford's brake demands that it previously got from its own sales force. The brake supplier can better schedule its own production and reduce the size of its own inventory.

The reengineering of procurement at Ford illustrates another characteristic of a true reengineering effort: Ford's changes would have been impossible without modern *information technology*—which is likewise true for the reengineering effort at IBM Credit. The new processes at both companies are not just the old processes with new wrinkles. They are entirely new processes that could not exist without today's information technology.

In the reengineered procurement process, for example, Ford's receiving clerk could not authorize vendor payment when goods arrived without the on-line database of purchase orders. In fact, absent the database, the receiving clerk would be just as much in the dark as ever about what goods Ford had actually ordered. The clerk's only option when goods arrived would have been, as previously, to assume that they had been ordered, accept them, and leave it to accounts payable to reconcile the receiving document, the purchase order, and the invoice. In theory, purchasing could have sent a photocopy of every purchase order to every receiving dock in the company, and receiving clerks could have checked arriving goods against these, but for obvious reasons such a paper-based system would prove impractical. Technology has enabled Ford to create a radically new mode of operation. Similarly, at IBM Credit, technology permits generalists to have easy access to information previously available only to specialists.

We say that in reengineering, information technology acts as an *essential enabler*. Without information technology, the process could not be reengineered. We will return to this theme in Chapter 5.

Example: Kodak

Another example of reengineering is the product development process that Kodak created in response to a competitive challenge. In 1987, Kodak's arch-rival, Fuji, announced a new 35mm, single-use camera, the sort that the customer buys loaded with film, uses once, and then returns to the manufacturer, who processes the film and breaks down the camera into parts for reuse. Kodak had no competitive offering, nor even one in the works, and its traditional product design process would have taken seventy weeks to produce a rival to Fuji's camera. Such a time delay would have handed Fuji an enormous head start and advantage in a new market. To slash its time-to-market, Kodak reengineered its product development process.

Most product development processes are either sequential, which makes them slow, or parallel, which also makes them slow, but for a different reason. In a sequential development process, individuals or groups working on one part of a product wait until the previous step is completed before beginning their own. Camera body designers, for example, may do their work first, followed by shutter designers, then the film advance mechanism designers, and so on. It is no mystery why this process is slow.

In a parallel design process, all the parts are designed simultaneously and integrated at the end. But this method engenders its own problem: Usually, the subsystems will not fit together because, even though all the groups were working from the same basic camera design, changes—often improvements—occurred along the way but were not communicated to the other groups. Then, when the camera is supposed to be ready to go to production, it's back to square one in design.

Kodak's old product development process was partly sequential and partly parallel but entirely slow. Designing the camera was conducted in parallel, with that method's attendant problems, and the design of the manufacturing tooling was tacked on, sequentially, at the end. At Kodak, the manufacturing engineers did not even begin their work until twenty-eight weeks after the product designers had started.

Kodak reengineered its product development process through the innovative use of a technology called CAD/CAM—Computer Aided Design/Computer Aided Manufacturing. This technology allows engineers to design at computer workstations instead of at drafting tables. Just working at a screen instead of on paper would have made the designers individually more productive, but such use of the technology would have had only marginal effect on the process as a whole.

The technology that has enabled Kodak to reengineer its process is an integrated product design database. Each day this database collects each engineer's work and combines all the individual efforts into a coherent whole. Each morning, design groups and individuals inspect the database to see whether someone else's work yesterday has created a problem for them or for the overall design. If so, they resolve the problem *immediately*, instead of after weeks or months of wasted work. Moreover, this technology permits manufacturing engineers to begin their tooling design just ten weeks into the development process, as soon as the product designers have given the first prototype some shape.

Kodak's new process, called concurrent engineering, has been used widely in the aerospace and automotive industries and is now starting to attract adherents in consumer goods companies. Kodak exploited concurrent engineering to cut nearly in half—to thirty-eight weeks—the time required to move the 35mm, single-use camera from concept to production. Furthermore, because the reengineered process allows tooling designers to get involved before product design is finished, their expertise can be tapped to create a design that is more easily and inexpensively manufactured. Kodak has reduced its tooling and manufacturing costs for the single-use camera by 25 percent.

In these three examples, we have seen illustrations of true *business reengineering*, even though some of them occurred before we had coined the term. These examples illustrate the four requisite characteristics of a reengineering effort and fulfill the definition that reengineering is the *fundamental* rethinking and *radical* redesign of business *processes* to achieve *dramatic* improvements in critical, contemporary measures of performance, such as cost, quality, service, and speed.

Several themes, listed below, emerge in these three cases, which we will explore at greater length later in this book.

• Process orientation

The improvements that IBM Credit, Ford, and Kodak effected did not come about by attending to narrowly defined tasks and working within predefined organizational boundaries. Each was achieved by looking at an entire process—credit issuance, procurement, and product development—that cut across organizational boundaries.

• Ambition

Minor improvements would not have been sufficient in any of these situations. All three companies aimed for breakthroughs. In reengineering its accounts payable process, Ford, for example, skipped the 20 percent fix and went for the 80 percent solution.

• Rule-breaking

Each of these companies broke with old traditions as they reengineered their processes. Assumptions of specialization, sequentiality, and timing were deliberately abandoned.

• Creative use of information technology

The agent that enabled these companies to break their old rules and create new process models was modern information technology. Information technology acts as an enabler that allows organizations to do work in radically different ways.

WHAT REENGINEERING ISN'T

People with hearsay knowledge of reengineering and those just being introduced to the concept often jump to the conclusion that it is much the same as other business improvement programs with which they are already familiar. "Oh, I get it. Reengineering," they may say, "is another name for downsizing." Or they equate it with restructuring or some other business fix of the month. Not at all. Reengineering has little or nothing in common with any of these other programs and differs in significant ways even from those with which it does share some common premises.

First, despite the prominent role played by information technology in business reengineering, it should by now be clear that reengineering is not the same as automation. Automating existing processes with information technology is analogous to paving cow paths. Automation simply provides more efficient ways of doing the wrong kinds of things.

Nor should people confuse business reengineering with so-called software reengineering, which means rebuilding obsolete information systems with more modern technology. Software reengineering often produces nothing more than sophisticated computerized systems that automate obsolete processes.

Reengineering is not restructuring or downsizing. These are just fancy terms for reducing capacity to meet current, lower demand. When the market wants fewer GM cars, GM reduces its size to better match demand. But downsizing and restructuring only mean doing less with less. Reengineering, by contrast, means doing *more* with less.

Reengineering also is not the same as reorganizing, delayering, or flattening an organization, although reengineering may, in fact, produce a flatter organization. As we have argued above, the problems facing companies do not result from their *organizational* structures but their *process* structures. Overlaying a new organization on top of an old process is pouring soured wine into new bottles.

Companies that earnestly set out to "bust" bureaucracies are holding the wrong end of the stick. Bureaucracy is not the problem. On the contrary, bureaucracy has been the solution for the last two hundred years. If you dislike bureaucracy in your company, try getting by without it. Chaos will result. Bureaucracy is the glue that holds traditional corporations together. The underlying problem, to which bureaucracy has been and remains a solution, is that of fragmented processes. The way to eliminate bureaucracy and flatten the organization is by reengineering the processes so that they are no longer fragmented. Then the company can manage nicely without its bureaucracy.

Nor is reengineering the same as quality improvement, total quality management (TQM), or any other manifestation of the contemporary quality movement. To be sure, quality programs and reengineering share a number of common themes. They both recognize the importance of processes, and they both start with the needs of the process customer and work backwards from there. However, the two programs also differ fundamentally. Quality programs work within the framework of a company's existing processes and seek to enhance them by means of what the Japanese call *kaizen*, or continuous incremental improvement. The aim is to do what we already do, only to do it better. Quality improvement seeks steady incremental improvement to process performance. Reengineering, as we have seen, seeks break-throughs, not by enhancing existing processes, but by discarding them and replacing them with entirely new ones. Reengineering involves, as well, a different approach to change management from that needed by quality programs.

Finally, we can do no better than to return to our original two-word definition for reengineering: starting over. Reengineering is about beginning again with a clean sheet of paper. It is about rejecting the conventional wisdom and received assumptions of the past. Reengineering is about inventing new approaches to process structure that bear little or no resemblance to those of previous eras.

Fundamentally, reengineering is about reversing the industrial revolution. Reengineering rejects the assumptions inherent in Adam Smith's industrial paradigm—the division of labor, economies of scale, hierarchical control, and all the other appurtenances of an early-stage developing economy. Reengineering is the search for new models of organizing work. Tradition counts for nothing. Reengineering is a new beginning.

CHAPTER 3

RETHINKING BUSINESS PROCESSES

It should be clear by now that a reengineered business process looks vastly different from a traditional process. But what, exactly, does a reengineered process *look like?*

We can't give a single answer to this question, because reengineered processes take many different forms. Nonetheless, we can say a great deal about the characteristics that typify reengineered processes.

As we've observed and participated in reengineering projects at dozens of corporations, we've noticed striking similarities among their various reengineered processes, similarities that transcend industry type and even the identity of the particular process. Much of what holds true for an auto company that has reengineered its processes is also true for an insurance company or a retailer.

That recurring themes appear in companies that have undergone reengineering should not come as a surprise, since the shape of a company that has reengineered, like the shape of the traditional industrial organization, flows from a small set of fundamental premises. The industrial model rests on the basic premise that workers have few skills and little time or capacity for training. This premise inevitably requires that the jobs and tasks assigned to these workers be very simple. Moreover, Adam Smith argued that people work most efficiently when they have only one easily understood task to perform. Simple tasks, though, demand complex processes to knit them all together, and for two hundred years companies have accepted the inconvenience, inefficiencies, and costs associated with complex processes in order to reap the benefits of simple tasks.

In reengineering, we stand the industrial model on its head. We say that in order to meet the contemporary demands of quality, service, flexibility, and low cost, processes must be kept simple. This need for simplicity has enormous consequences for how processes are designed and organizations are shaped.

Here, then, are some commonalities, some recurring themes or characteristics, that we frequently encounter in reengineered business processes.

- Several jobs are combined into one

The most basic and common feature of reengineered processes is the absence of an assembly line; that is, many formerly distinct jobs or tasks are integrated and compressed into one. We observed this characteristic at IBM Credit, where several specialist jobs such as credit checker or pricer were combined into a single position, "deal structurer." We encountered a similar transformation at an electronics company that had reengineered its order fulfillment process. Previously, specialists located in separate organizations performed each of the five steps between selling and installing the company's equipment. Because this process involved so many handoffs, errors and misunderstandings were inevitable—all the more so because no one individual or group had responsibility for, or knowledge of, the entire process. When customers telephoned with problems, no one could help them.

In reengineering this process, the company compressed responsibility for the various steps and assigned it to one person, the "customer service representative." That person now performs the whole process and also serves as the single point of contact for the customer. Our term for such an individual responsible for an end-to-end process is *case worker*.

It is not always possible to compress all of the steps in a lengthy process into one integrated job performed by a single person. In some situations (product delivery, for example), the various steps must be performed in different locations. In those instances, a company needs several people, each managing parts of the process. In other cases, it may not prove practical to teach one person all the skills he or she would need to perform the entire process.

Bell Atlantic, for example, found that it was too much to ask one person to handle all the tasks involved in establishing high-speed, digital circuits for business customers. But the company also wanted to do away with the problems that inevitably occurred when the order was passed between people across departmental lines. To eliminate the handoffs, Bell Atlantic organized what we call a *case team*, a group of people who have among them all the skills that are needed to handle an installation order.

Case team members—who previously were located in different departments at several geographic locations—were brought together into a single unit and given total responsibility for installing the equipment. While handoffs between team members may still create some delays and errors, they are insignificant compared to the problems that the cross-organizational handoffs caused. Perhaps most important, everyone now knows who has responsibility for getting an order processed quickly and accurately.

The payoffs of integrated processes, case workers, and case teams can be enormous. Eliminating handoffs means doing away with the errors, delays, and rework that they engender. Typically, a case worker-based process operates *ten times* faster than the assembly line version that it replaces. Bell Atlantic, for example, reduced the time it takes to install a high-speed digital service link from thirty days to three; in some instances, it now takes only several hours. Moreover, because the new process generates fewer errors and misunderstandings, the company doesn't need additional people to find and fix them.

Integrated processes also have reduced process administration overheads. Because employees involved in the process assume responsibility for making sure that customers' requirements are met on time and with no defects, they need less supervision. Instead, the company encourages these empowered employees to find innovative and creative ways to reduce cycle time and cost continually while producing a defect-free product or service. Improved control is another benefit of integrated processes; because they involve fewer people, assigning responsibility for them and monitoring performance is easier.

• Workers make decisions

Companies that undertake reengineering, not only compress processes horizontally by having case workers or case teams perform multiple, sequential tasks but vertically as well. Vertical compression means that at the points in a process where workers used to have to go up the managerial hierarchy for an answer, they now make their own decisions. Instead of separating decision-making from real work, decision-making becomes *part* of the work. Workers themselves now do that portion of a job that, formerly, managers performed.

Under the mass-production paradigm, the tacit assumption is that the people actually performing work have neither the time nor the inclination to monitor and control it and that they lack the depth and breadth of knowledge required to make decisions about it. The industrial practice of building hierarchical management structures follows from this assumption. Accountants, auditors, and supervisors check, record, and monitor work. Managers supervise the worker bees and handle the exceptions. This assumption, and its consequences, need to be discarded.

The benefits of compressing work vertically as well as horizontally include fewer delays, lower overhead costs, better customer response, and greater empowerment for workers.

• The steps in the process are performed in a natural order

Reengineering processes are freed from the tyranny of straight-line sequence; natural precedence in the work, rather than the artificial one introduced by linearity, can be exploited. Typically, in a conventional process, person 1 must complete task 1 before passing the results to person 2 to do task 2. But what if task 2 could be performed simultaneously with task 1? Linear sequencing of tasks imposes an artificial precedence that slows work down.

In reengineered processes, work is sequenced in terms of what *needs* to follow what. In one manufacturing company, for example, it took five steps to go from the receipt of a customer order to the installation of the equipment. The first step was to determine the customer's requirements; the second, to translate them into internal product codes; the third, to convey the coded information to various plants and warehouses; the fourth, to receive and assemble the components; and the fifth, to deliver and install the equipment. A different organization performed each step.

Traditionally, group 1 completed step 1 before group 2 began step 2, but this was not actually necessary. The employee responsible for step 1 spent most of her time gathering information that would not be required until step 5. Because of the arbitrary linear sequencing imposed on the process, however, no one could begin working on step 2 until step 1 was completed. In the reengineered version of this process, step 2 begins as soon as step 1 has collected enough information to get it started. Then while steps 2, 3, and 4 operate, step 1 continues to collect the information needed for step 5. As a result, the company reduced the time it takes to fill a customer order by more than 60 percent.

We have already encountered another example of a process freed from strict linearity with Kodak's new product development process. There, design of the manufacturing tooling does not have to wait until product design is finished. As soon as the basic product design is in place, tooling engineers can not only begin their work, they can influence the rest of the product design process.

"Delinearizing" processes speeds them up in two ways. First, many jobs get done simultaneously. Second, reducing the amount of time that elapses between the early and late steps of a process narrows the window for major change that might make the earlier work obsolete or make the later work inconsistent with the earlier. Organizations thereby encounter less rework, which is another major source of delay.

• Processes have multiple versions

We might term the fourth common characteristic of reengineered processes the end of standardization. Traditional processes were intended to provide mass production for a mass market. All inputs were handled identically, so companies could produce uniform and consistent outputs. In a world of diverse and changing markets that logic is obsolete. To meet the demands of today's environment, we need multiple versions of the *same* process, each one tuned to the requirements of different markets, situations, or inputs. What's more, these new processes must have the same economies of scale that result from mass production.

Processes with multiple versions or paths usually begin with a "triage" step to determine which version works best in a given situation. Triage is at work at IBM Credit, which has put in place three versions of the credit issuance process: one for straightforward cases (which are performed entirely by computer), one for medium hard cases (performed by the deal structurer), and one for difficult cases (performed by the deal structurer with help from specialist advisers).

We know a man who, in order to make some minor improvement to his house, had to wait six months for a public hearing before a city board that, when it finally considered his application, took only twenty seconds to approve it. His application, illustrated by a hand-drawn sketch, had to travel through the same process as those of mega-million-dollar office tower developers with volumes of blueprints, plans, and materials specification sheets. If the city had reengineered its building permit system, it might have replaced the single process with two or maybe three processes: one for small projects, one for big projects, and one for those in the middle. Simple triage, based on some preestablished thresholds, would have sent our friend's application quickly and efficiently through the right one.

Traditional one-size-fits-all processes are usually very complex, since they must incorporate special procedures and exceptions to handle a wide range of situations. A multi-version process, by contrast, is clean and simple, because each version needs to handle only the cases for which it is appropriate. There are no special cases and exceptions.

• Work is performed where it makes the most sense

A fifth recurring theme in reengineered processes is the shifting of work across organizational boundaries. In traditional organizations, work is organized around specialists—and not just on the factory floor. Accountants know how to count, and purchasing clerks know how to order things. So when the accounting department needs new pencils, the purchasing department buys them. Purchasing finds vendors, negotiates price, places the order, inspects the goods, and pays the invoice—and eventually the accountants get their pencils, unless the approved supplier is short on pencils and purchasing decides to substitute pens.

This kind of process is expensive, since it involves a variety of departments plus the overhead that's associated with tracking all the paper and fitting all the pieces of the process together. One company we know ran a controlled experiment and learned that it expended $100 in internal costs to buy $3 worth of batteries. It also discovered that 35 percent of its purchase orders were for amounts less than $500.

The notion of spending $100 internally to expend $500 or less did not sit well, so the company decided to off-load the responsibility for purchasing goods onto the process customers; in other words, the accountants—as well as everyone else—now buy their own pencils. They know from whom to buy and what to pay, because purchasing has negotiated these prices and given the accountants a list of approved vendors. Each operating unit has a credit card with a $500 credit limit. At the end of the month, the bank that issued the credit card sends the manufacturer a tape of all the card transactions, which the company then runs against its internal general ledger system, so that the accountants' budget gets charged for their pencils.

As a result, the requesters receive their products more quickly and with less hassle, and the company spends far less than $100 on the processing costs. This example illustrates what we mean when we say that the customer of a process can perform some or all of the process in order to eliminate handoffs and overhead and cut costs.

In an analogous way, an electronics equipment manufacturer reengineered its field service process by shifting some of the repair work to its customers, who now make simple fixes themselves without having to wait for a technician to arrive with, maybe, the right spare parts. Some spare parts are now stored at each customer's site and managed through a computerized parts management system. When a problem crops up, the customer calls the manufacturer's field service hot line and describes the symptoms to a diagnostician, who can ask a computer for help. If the problem is something the customer can fix, the diagnostician tells the customer what part to replace and how to install it. Later, the manufacturer picks up the old part and leaves a new part in its place. Service technicians make site calls only when the problem is too complex for the customer.

Sometimes, though, it's more effective when the supplier to a customer process performs some or all of the process on behalf of the customer. Navistar International, for example, has shifted some of its work back to its suppliers. Instead of managing its own warehouse inventory of tires to be installed on the trucks it manufactures, Navistar has turned warehouse management over to Goodyear, which has more expertise than Navistar at managing tire warehouses. Goodyear sees that Navistar gets the Goodyear, Bridgestone, and Michelin tires it needs as it needs them.

For Navistar, this shift is the ultimate in process simplification: The manufacturer no longer has to manage its tire inventory at all. Since Goodyear, the supplier, is much better than Navistar, the customer, at warehouse management, the amount of inventory in the warehouse has dropped from twenty-two days' supply to five.

In other words, in the aftermath of reengineering, the correspondence between processes and organizations may look very different from how it looked beforehand. Work is shifted across organizational boundaries to improve overall process performance. Much of the work done in organizations consists of integrating related pieces of work that independent organizational units perform. Relocating work across organizational boundaries, as exemplified in the cases above, eliminates the need for this integration.

• Checks and controls are reduced

Another kind of nonvalue-adding work that gets minimized in reengineered processes is checking and control; or, to put it more precisely, reengineered processes use controls only to the extent that they make economic sense.

Conventional processes are replete with checking and control steps, which add no value but are included to ensure that people aren't abusing the process. In a typical purchasing process, for example, the purchasing department checks the signature of the person requesting an item to make sure that person is authorized to acquire the requisitioned goods in the dollar amount specified and verify that the department's budget is good for the bill. All this checking is to make sure that people in the organization are not buying items that they should not.

While that objective may be laudable, many organizations fail to recognize the costs associated with strict control. It takes time and labor to do all this checking; in fact, it may take more time and effort to do the checking than to do the actual purchasing. Worse, the cost of the checking may even exceed the cost of the goods being purchased.

Reengineered processes exhibit a more balanced approach. Instead of tightly checking work as it is performed, reengineered processes often have aggregate or deferred controls. These control systems will, by design, tolerate modest and limited abuse, by delaying the point at which abuse is detected or by examining aggregate patterns rather than individual instances. The reengineered control systems, however, more than compensate for any possible increase in abuse by dramatically lowering the costs and other encumbrances associated with the control itself.

Consider the credit card–based purchasing process we just described. Compared to more traditional processes, this one seems almost devoid of controls. Departments might use their credit cards to go on wild spending sprees. People could run away to Brazil with the spoils of their raids on office supply vendors. Or so

feared the company's internal auditors. But they were wrong because the reengineered purchasing process does have a point of
control; unauthorized purchases will be detected when the credit
card tape is run against the department's budget and when the
departmental manager reviews the expenditures. Given the credit
limit on the cards, the process designers felt it was better to swal-
low the limited exposure to abuse that the new process embodies in
order to eliminate the overhead cost associated with the traditional
controls. (We should keep in mind, as well, that the old process
was far from immune to abuse.)

Some automobile insurance companies are taking approaches
similar to the one we just described in their claims processing
activities. Traditionally, insurers dispatch claims adjusters and ap-
praisers to assess the extent of auto damage and determine how
much the insurer is willing to pay for repair. This control step is
designed to make sure that the body shop performing the repair
doesn't inflate the bill or do unnecessary work. But adjusters aren't
inexpensive, and they slow the process down, thereby antagoniz-
ing claimants—and angry claimants often sue.

Consequently, some insurers take adjusters out of the process
for small accidents. They send the claimant to an approved body
shop and say they will pay for whatever needs to be done. How do
they avoid overbilling? By periodically reviewing the body shop's
charges, the insurer can get a sense of the pattern of its repairs and
compare them against normative standards and patterns of other
body shops. A shop that is doing too many front-end alignments,
say, will get a warning: If you continue this abuse, you'll get
dropped from the approved list, and you'll receive no more refer-
rals from us. The insurance companies are happy to accept the
potential of some short-term abuse, because the cost will be more
than offset by the benefits of a streamlined claims process that is
less expensive to operate and leaves claimants happy.

• Reconciliation is minimized

Yet another form of nonvalue-adding work that reengineered
processes minimize is reconciliation. They do it by cutting back the
number of external contact points that a process has, thereby

reducing the chances that inconsistent data requiring reconciliation will be received. The accounts payable process at Ford, described in Chapter 2, illustrates this principle.

Ford's old accounts payable process contained three points of contact with vendors: at the purchasing department through the purchase order, at the receiving dock through the receiving paperwork, and at accounts payable through the invoice. Three points of contact meant enormous opportunities for inconsistency; the purchase order could disagree with either the receiving document or the invoice, and either of them could disagree with the other. By eliminating the invoice, Ford reduced the points of external contact from three to two and the opportunity for inconsistency by two-thirds. As a result, the checking and reconciliation work that accounts payable had heretofore performed became unnecessary, which meant that the accounts payable organization could shrink dramatically.

This theme and several others are illustrated in the way Wal-Mart, working with Procter & Gamble, reengineered the management of its Pampers inventory. Pampers, a disposable diaper, is a bulky item that requires a lot of storage space relative to its dollar value. Wal-Mart maintained Pampers inventory at its distribution centers, from which it filled orders coming from the stores. When the distribution center inventory began to run low, Wal-Mart would reorder more diapers from P&G.

Managing inventory is a delicate balancing act. Too little inventory makes for unhappy customers and lost sales. Too much incurs high financing and storage costs. Not only that, inventory management is itself a costly activity. With the idea of improving this aspect of its business, Wal-Mart approached P&G with the observation that P&G probably knew more about diaper movement through warehouses than Wal-Mart, as it had information about usage patterns and reorders from retailers all over the country. Wal-Mart suggested, therefore, that P&G should assume the responsibility of telling Wal-Mart when to reorder Pampers for its distribution center and in what quantity. Every day, Wal-Mart would tell P&G how much stock it was moving out of the distribution center to the stores. When P&G felt it was appropriate, it would tell Wal-Mart that it was time to reorder and how much. If the recommendation seemed to make sense, Wal-Mart would approve it, and P&G would ship the goods.

The new arrangement worked so well that over time Wal-Mart suggested that P&G henceforth skip the purchase recommendations and just ship the diapers it thought Wal-Mart would need. In other words, Wal-Mart off-loaded its inventory replenishment function onto its supplier, illustrating the principle of relocating work across organizational boundaries that we discussed earlier. In this case, though, the boundaries were *inter*company, not *intra*company. Both companies reap advantages.

Wal-Mart has eliminated the costs associated with maintaining its Pampers inventory. The stock is managed more effectively, since P&G indeed can do a better job than Wal-Mart. Therefore, the retailer has less inventory on hand and suffers fewer out-of-stock situations. Lower inventory levels frees up space in Wal-Mart's distribution center, and reduces the retailer's need for working capital to finance that inventory. In fact, inventory management is now so streamlined that goods move through Wal-Mart's distribution center and stores and into the hands of the consumer even before Wal-Mart has to pay P&G for the goods. When it does pay, Wal-Mart is using cash it has already received from consumers. Whether we call this arrangement negative inventory carrying costs or an infinite return on capital, it is a wonderful state of affairs for Wal-Mart.

Anyone could provide diapers to Wal-Mart, but P&G adds value to the diapers it supplies by performing the inventory management process. It thereby endears itself as a preferred supplier to the large retail chain. As a preferred supplier, P&G gets additional shelf space in Wal-Mart stores and the much sought after end-aisle displays. The reengineered process also has major *internal* performance benefits for P&G. First, the company can run its manufacturing and logistics operations more efficiently now that it has the information it needs to better project product demand. Inventory no longer moves to Wal-Mart irregularly in large lots, but continually in small ones. Other manufacturer-retailer combinations, such as Levi Strauss and many of its customers, also use this approach, known as "continuous replenishment."

The second benefit P&G reaps from its new arrangement with Wal-Mart relates back to the notion of minimizing the number of external contact points—in this case, in P&G's accounts receivable process. Conventionally, accounts receivable's job is to reconcile payments from customers with customer orders and with the vendor's own invoices. In principle they should match, but reality does not always follow principle. When they do not—as, for example, when prices have recently changed—these conflicts vanish into the black hole of reconciliation, where they consume enormous energy and damage the vendor-customer relationship. P&G, however, now has only two accounts receivable contacts with Wal-Mart, the invoice and the payment. Wal-Mart no longer generates the original order; P&G does. In this way, errors and the need for reconciliation are enormously reduced.

• A case manager provides a single point of contact

The use of someone we might call a "case manager" is another recurring characteristic we find in reengineered processes. This mechanism proves useful when the steps of a process either are so complex or are dispersed in such a way that integrating them for a single person or even a small team is impossible. Acting as a buffer between the still complex process and the customer, the case manager behaves with the customer as if he or she were responsible for performing the entire process, even though that is really not the case.

To perform this role—that is, to be able to answer the customer's questions and solve customer problems—the case manager needs access to all the information systems that the people actually performing the process use and the ability to contact those people with questions and requests for further assistance when necessary.

We sometimes call the case managers "empowered" customer service representatives to distinguish them from traditional CSRs, who are often people with skimpy information and less clout.

Empowered CSRs can actually get things done. At Duke Power Company, a large public utility based in Raleigh, North Carolina, case managers present customers with the useful fiction of an integrated customer service process by handling all their problems while shielding them from the real complexities of the actual process.

• Hybrid centralized/decentralized operations are prevalent

Companies that have reengineered their processes have the ability to combine the advantages of centralization and decentralization in the same process. We will encounter this theme at Hewlett-Packard in Chapter 5, where a standard purchasing system and a shared database allow the company to combine the best of both worlds.

Information technology increasingly enables companies to operate as though their individual units were fully autonomous, while the organization still enjoys the economies of scale that centralization creates. Equipping field sales representatives with notebook computers connected by wireless modems to the central office or to corporate headquarters, for instance, gives salespeople instant access to information that is maintained there. At the same time, controls incorporated into the software they use to write up sales contracts prevent the salespeople from quoting unreasonable prices or specifying delivery or other conditions that the organization cannot meet. With this technology, companies can reengineer the sales process so as to eliminate the bureaucratic machinery of regional field offices, enhance the sales representatives' autonomy and empowerment, and, simultaneously, improve the control the company has over selling prices and conditions.

Many banks have established separate divisions to sell different products to the same clients—large corporations, for instance. One division sells traditional lines of credit; another, asset-based finance; a third, letters of credit; and a fourth, pension fund management services. The decentralized structure ensures that each division focuses on the products and services with which it has the most expertise, and, simultaneously, promotes real entrepreneurial autonomy. It also guarantees chaos.

In this fractionalized structure, everyone is looking at narrow slices of the market, but no one is looking at the customer as a whole, so important aggregate issues may fall between the cracks. One bank, for example, established a $20 million credit limit for a certain customer and instructed each autonomous unit to enforce it. Each one did—by extending the client the full $20 million credit. The bank-wide exposure to the client was therefore many times that figure. Management only understood its true exposure after the client went bankrupt. To avoid these kinds of problems, several banks have implemented bank-wide customer databases that all operating units share. Every unit puts what they know about the customer and their relationship with that customer into the database, and every unit uses the database as a source of customer information. In this way, units with freedom to act independently can coordinate their activities without the bureaucratic interference of a central control point.

The objective of presenting the above examples and of pointing out the characteristics that we see recurring in reengineered business processes is not to suggest that all reengineered processes look the same or that process redesign is a straightforward matter. Nothing could be further from the truth. Not every reengineered business process will display all of the characteristics we have cited. Indeed, they could not, because some are conflicting. Actually creating a new design requires insight, creativity, and judgment. These ingredients are also needed for designing the jobs and organizations that support reengineered processes. It is to that topic we next turn our attention.

CHAPTER 4

THE NEW WORLD OF WORK

We have repeatedly made the point that reengineering entails the radical redesign of a company's business processes. But while reengineering does start with process redesign, it doesn't end there. Fundamental changes in business processes have implications for many other parts and aspects of an organization—every part of it, in fact.

When a process is reengineered, jobs evolve from narrow and task-oriented to multidimensional. People who once did as they were instructed now make choices and decisions on their own instead. Assembly-line work disappears. Functional departments lose their reasons for being. Managers stop acting like supervisors and behave more like coaches. Workers focus more on the customers' needs and less on their bosses'. Attitudes and values change in response to new incentives. Practically every aspect of the organization is transformed, often beyond recognition.

Let's look closer at the kinds of changes that occur when a company reengineers its business processes.

• Work units change—from functional departments to process teams

Companies that reengineer are, in effect, putting back together again the work that Adam Smith and Henry Ford broke into tiny pieces so many years ago. Once it is restructured, process teams—groups of people working together to perform an entire process—turn out to be the logical way to organize the people who perform the work. Process teams don't contain *representatives* from all the functional departments involved. Rather, process teams *replace* the old departmental structure. While there are several different kinds of process teams, we mean something very particular when we use the word "team."

Think of the progress of an order through an organization (or of a new product idea or an insurance claim). Each of these items gets handled by many different people, but those people are not organizationally integrated. They are scattered all over the company in functional silos—different departments, groups, divisions, and so on. This fractionation creates numerous problems, but in particular it promotes incongruent goals among the different people involved. One person might care about inventory turns while another is focused on delivery time.

An alternative approach is to look at the same collection of people who are now handling the order or new product or claim, but instead of separating them into departments, to put them together in a team. We aren't necessarily changing what they do, but we're arranging for them to do it together instead of separately, scattered all over the organization. In some sense we're only putting back together a group of workers who have been artificially separated by organization. When they're rejoined, we call them a process team. A process team, in other words, is a unit that naturally falls together to complete a whole piece of work—a process.

Process teams are of many sorts, the right one depending on the nature of the work being done. One we call a case team. Here, as we saw with Bell Atlantic in the last chapter, a number of people with different skills work together to complete routine, recurring work—such as processing an insurance claim or connecting a telephone customer to its long-distance carrier. In the past, when a Bell Atlantic business customer requested a connection between its telephone system and a long-distance carrier for data services, for instance, the request traveled from department to department at Bell Atlantic, taking from two weeks to one month to complete its journey. In reengineering that process, Bell Atlantic took people from many functional departments and put them together in case teams, which now handle most customer requests in a matter of days or even hours instead of weeks. Because case teams perform recurring work—that is, they process similar customer requests day after day—the people on the team are usually permanently grouped together. (We will look more closely at the Bell Atlantic example in Chapter 13.)

Another kind of a process team has a shorter life span, because it stays together only for as long as it takes to complete a particular, episodic task. We call these virtual teams. Kodak's new product design process, for instance, requires many people with diverse talents—shutter designers, lens specialists, manufacturing experts, and others—to work jointly on a new camera design project. When the camera is designed and goes into production, however, the project is finished and the virtual team dissolves, its members moving on to other projects and other teams. People may simultaneously be members of more than one virtual team, splitting their time among different projects.

IBM Credit (which we first looked at in Chapter 2) uses a third kind of process team. It's like a case team, but it consists of only one person. Prior to reengineering, when IBM Credit put together a financing package for a prospective customer, credit checking was done in the credit department, pricing was done in the pricing department, other terms and conditions were set in the business practices department, and the final offer got pulled together by someone in the bid preparation department. People in these departments passed the work back and forth among themselves, with all the usual errors and delays. But when the company reengineered its deal structuring process, it integrated those four separate functions, replacing four departments with one. Many of the people—called deal structurers—who staff this new department are the same people who used to be specialists.

IBM Credit went further than simply grouping four specialists into a process team. Now, each individual can shepherd an entire deal through the process from beginning to end. IBM Credit realized that one trained person with access to on-line data could handle 90 percent or more of the work that used to get handed off among specialists. A few specialist advisers assigned to assist deal structurers could help them handle the rest. At IBM Credit, the process team is a team of one—what we have called a case worker.

• Jobs change—from simple tasks to multi-dimensional work

People working on process teams will find their work far different from the jobs to which they've been accustomed. Assembly-line work, whether it's of the white- or blue-collar variety, is highly specialized—the repetitious performance of one task. The job may require some training—how to insert a particular component into a particular printed circuit board, for instance. It may even require extensive education—a college degree in mechanical engineering in order to design camera shutters. But when they're doing task work, neither the assembly-line worker nor the mechanical engineer needs to know—or even cares much about—the whole process of, say, building a computer or developing a camera design.

Process team workers, who are collectively responsible for process results rather than individually responsible for tasks, have a different kind of job. They share joint responsibility with their team members for performing the whole process, not just a small piece of it. They not only use a broader range of skills from day to day, they have to be thinking of a far bigger picture. While not every member of the team will be doing exactly the same work— after all, they have different skills and abilities—the lines between them blur. Each team member will have at least a basic familiarity with all the steps in the process and is likely to perform several of them. Moreover, everything an individual does is imbued with an appreciation for the process as a whole.

A clear example of how jobs change after reengineering is provided by IBM Credit. The old jobs consisted of specialists who did one task. The new deal structurers perform a variety of tasks. They are generalists. Their work is multidimensional.

What happened at Kodak when the company reengineered its product design process? A lens designer who used to concentrate strictly and narrowly on lens design now designs lenses in the context of the camera as a whole, which means that he or she inevitably contributes to other aspects of the design and that his or her own design will be influenced by what others have to say. The lens no longer operates strictly within the limits of one designer. The job has become multi-dimensional.

Sometimes process reengineering shifts the boundaries between different kinds of work. At one company, for instance, engineers who previously had prepared data for other people to use in producing marketing brochures now produce the marketing brochures themselves; they know more about the product than the marketing people, and they are able to use the desktop publishing tools themselves. The marketing people now act as advisers to the engineers. Work for both groups—the engineers and the marketing people—has broadened.

As work becomes more multi-dimensional, it also becomes more substantive. Reengineering eliminates not just waste but non-value-adding work as well. Most of the checking, reconciling, waiting, monitoring, tracking—the unproductive work that exists because of boundaries within an organization and to compensate for process fragmentation—is eliminated by reengineering, which means that people will spend more time doing *real* work.

After reengineering, work becomes more satisfying, since workers achieve a greater sense of completion, closure, and accomplishment from their jobs. They actually perform a whole job—a process or a subprocess—that by definition produces a result that somebody cares about. Process performers share many of the challenges and rewards of entrepreneurs. They are focused on customers whose satisfaction is their aim. They're not just trying to keep the boss happy or to work through the bureaucracy.

Moreover, work becomes more rewarding since people's jobs have a greater component of growth and learning. In a process team environment, personal development does not mean climbing up through the hierarchy but expanding one's breadth—learning more so one can encompass a larger part of the process. After reengineering there is no such thing as "mastering" a job; as a worker's expertise and experience grow, his or her job grows with it.

Moreover, since workers in reengineered processes spend more time on value-adding work and less time on work that adds no value, their contributions to the company increase, and, consequently, jobs in a reengineered environment will on the whole be more highly compensated.

There is, however, a challenging side to all this good news about work in a reengineered environment. If jobs are more satisfying, they are also more challenging and difficult. Much of the old, routine work is eliminated or automated. If the old model was simple tasks for simple people, the new one is complex jobs for smart people, which raises the bar for entry into the workforce. Few simple, routine, unskilled jobs are to be found in a reengineered environment.

- People's roles change—from controlled to empowered

A task-oriented, traditional company hires people and expects them to follow the rules. Companies that have reengineered don't want employees who can follow rules; they want people who will make their own rules. As management invests teams with the responsibility of completing an entire process, it must also give them the authority to make the decisions needed to get it done.

The following example illustrates the nature and payoff of empowerment. A guest approached the doorman at a major hotel and complained that his radar detector had been stolen from his car in the hotel's garage. The doorman, empowered to perform customer service, asked how much it cost, took the guest to the front desk, and commanded "Give this man $150" to the clerk. Everybody gulped, but the customer was satisfied. Two weeks later, the general manager received a letter from this customer that stated he had found his radar detector in his trunk. In the envelope was also a check for $150. The postscript to the letter added: "By the way, I will never stay at any other hotel chain for the rest of my life."

People working in a reengineered process are, of necessity, empowered. As process team workers they are both permitted and required to think, interact, use judgment, and make decisions. At IBM Credit and Kodak, intrusive supervisors and managers have no place in the reengineered work processes. Imagine an IBM Credit deal structurer who is trying to handle several cases in different stages of completion and to get as many of them done as quickly as possible. Suddenly, a supervisor appears to check on his or her progress. Real work screeches to a halt while the deal structurer shifts to satisfying the supervisor instead of the customer. At Kodak, when could the head of the lens department "approve" the lens design? The lens design isn't final until the camera design is done. Supervisory approval would only slow the process.

Teams, of one person or several, performing process-oriented work are inevitably self-directing. Within the boundaries of their obligations to the organization—agreed upon deadlines, productivity goals, quality standards, etc.—they decide how and when work is going to be done. If they have to wait for supervisory direction of their tasks, they aren't process teams.

Empowerment is an unavoidable consequence of reengineered processes; processes can't be reengineered without empowering process workers. Consequently, companies that reengineer must consider additional criteria in their hiring. It is no longer enough merely to look at prospective employees' education, training, and skills; their *character* becomes an issue as well. Are they self-starting? Do they have self-discipline? Are they motivated to do what it takes to please a customer?

Reengineering and its consequent empowerment have powerful implications for the kinds of people companies will hire.

• Job preparation changes—from training to education

If jobs in reengineered processes require that people not follow rules, but rather that they exercise judgment in order to do the right thing, then employees need sufficient education so that they can discern for themselves what that right thing is. Traditional companies typically stress employee *training*—teaching workers how to perform a particular job or how to handle one specific situation or another. In companies that have reengineered, the emphasis shifts from training to *education*—or to hiring the educated. Training increases skills and competence and teaches employees the "how" of a job. Education increases their insight and understanding and teaches the "why."

Hill's Pet Products, a subsidiary of Colgate-Palmolive, recently built a new plant in Richmond, Indiana, at which the company has implemented many of the principles of reengineered processes. The company's management knew the kind of people they needed to work on the plant floor and set out to hire 150 of them. The company received thousands of applications and the personnel department looked closely at 3,000. When the finalists were selected, practically all of them shared one characteristic: They lacked factory work experience. The applicants who the company wanted mostly turned out to be former schoolteachers, police officers, and others who had the right character and the right education although they lacked factory skills. But that ostensible deficit wasn't a major problem. The company was able to train the new hires, because these were people who already knew how to learn.

For multi-dimensional and changing jobs, companies don't need people to fill a slot, because the slot will be only roughly defined. Companies need people who can figure out what the job takes and do it, people who can create the slot that fits them. Moreover, the slot will keep changing. In an environment of flexibility and change, it is clearly impossible to hire people who already know everything they're ever going to need to know, so continuing education over the lifetime of a job becomes the norm in a reengineered company.

• Focus of performance measures and compensation shifts— from activity to results

Worker compensation in traditional companies is relatively straightforward: People are paid for their time. In a traditional operation—whether it's on an assembly line manufacturing machines or in a clerical office processing paperwork—an individual employee's work has no quantifiable value. What, for instance, is the dollar value of a soldered joint? Or of verified employment data on an insurance application form? Neither is worth anything by itself. Only the finished car or the newly-issued insurance policy has value to the company. When work is fragmented into simple tasks, companies have no choice but to measure workers on the efficiency with which they perform narrowly defined work. The trouble is that increased efficiency of narrowly defined tasks does not necessarily translate into improved process performance.

In contrast, the IBM Credit deal structurer is not measured by how many pieces of paper he or she handles but by the number and profitability of finalized deals and by their quality, as reflected in customer satisfaction surveys. When employees are performing process work, companies can measure their performance and pay them on the basis of the value they create. That value is measurable because in reengineered business processes, teams create products or services that have intrinsic value. A new camera, for instance, has value; a shutter mechanism does not.

Reengineering also forces companies to reconsider some basic assumptions about compensation. For instance, an employee's performance in a reengineered job this year does not guarantee anything about his or her performance in the years to come. For that reason, base salaries in companies with reengineered processes tend to remain relatively flat after adjustments for inflation. Substantial rewards for outstanding performance take the form of bonuses, not pay raises.

Other compensation assumptions also fall away after reengineering: paying people based on job rank or seniority; paying people just for showing up; and giving people a raise just because another year has passed.

Paying people based on their position in the organization—the higher up they are, the more money they make—is inconsistent with the principles of reengineering. Traditional point schemes, in which the size of a person's salary is a function of the number of subordinates that person has working for him or her and the size of his or her budget, also don't fit in a process-oriented environment. Finely graded hierarchies with a lot of positions—analyst 1, analyst 2, senior analyst, etc.—each with a narrow compensation band, must be discarded.

In companies that have reengineered, contribution and performance are the primary bases for compensation. Precedents for this approach exist: Even in traditional companies, the vice president of sales is rarely the most highly paid person in the sales organization—that honor usually belongs to the most productive sales rep. On Wall Street, the chairman of an investment bank is typically not the most highly paid individual; rather, it is usually the star bond dealer or currency trader.

In companies that have reengineered, performance is measured by value created and compensation should be set accordingly.

• Advancement criteria change—from performance to ability

A bonus is the appropriate reward for a job well done. Advancement to a new job is not. In the aftermath of reengineering, the distinction between advancement and performance is firmly drawn. Advancement to another job within the organization is a function of ability, not performance. It is a change, not a reward.

Progressive Insurance considers this distinction important enough to note in the company's annual report. "One of our core principles," the document says, "is that we pay for performance and promote for ability." Once considered, the principle seems obvious. But it is rarely followed. If Elizabeth is a good chemist, conventional thinking goes, she will be a good manager of chemists. Often that isn't true, and Elizabeth's "promotion" could get the company a bad manager at the cost of a good chemist.

Capital Holding's Direct Response Group, an insurer, makes the distinction between performance and advancement quite clear to its employees. "We've separated the results review, at which we reward people with compensation, from the development review," says DRG senior vice president Pamela Godwin. "This way, we can even get people who may have delivered outstanding results to acknowledge their need for additional growth and development. By separating the two evaluations we help keep the differences clear in employees' minds."

• Values change—from protective to productive

Reengineering entails as great a shift in the culture of an organization as in its structural configuration. Reengineering demands that employees deeply believe that they work for their customers, not for their bosses. They will believe this only to the extent that the company's practices of reward reinforce it. For instance, Xerox Corporation doesn't just tell its people that customers pay their salaries, it makes the connection explicit. The company now bases a major portion of every manager's bonus on a measure of customer satisfaction. When their bonuses depended solely on how well their individual departments performed, managers continually warred with one another over fault, jurisdiction, and resources. Now, the internal arguments have all but disappeared as managers have shifted their focus to maximizing customer satisfaction.

An organization's management systems—the ways in which people are paid, the measures by which their performance is evaluated, and so forth—are the primary shapers of employees' values and beliefs.

Unfortunately, too many managers still believe that all they have to do to shape their employees' belief systems is to articulate some high-sounding values and then make speeches about them. Creating a corporate value statement alone is useless and just another faddish exercise. Without supporting management systems, most corporate value statements are collections of empty platitudes that only increase organizational cynicism. To be worth the paper it's printed on, a value statement must be reinforced by the company's management systems. The statement articulates values; the management systems give those values life and reality within the company.

And, of course, senior management must live these values themselves. If an executive says it's important to care about customers and then spends an hour a week on the phone with customers, the value of that time to customers may be minor, but its value to the organization is immeasurable. The hour is a symbol and a demonstration of management's personal commitment to the values by which they expect everyone to live.

The cultural values found in some traditional companies are the byproducts of fragmented management systems, which focus on past performance, emphasize control, and enshrine the hierarchy. Whatever such a company's value statement might *say*, its management systems may in fact promote values something like this:

—My boss pays my salary: For all the talk about serving customers, the real objective is to keep the boss happy.

—I'm just a cog in the wheel: My best strategy is to keep my head down and not make waves.

—The more direct reports I have, the more important I am: The one with the biggest empire wins.

—Tomorrow will be just like today: It always has been.

The trouble is that these values and beliefs do not promote the performance that customer-oriented organizations require. They are inconsistent with the new processes created in a reengineered environment; and unless the values change, new processes, no matter how well designed, will never work. Changing values is as important a part of reengineering as changing processes.

In a company that has reengineered, employees must hold beliefs such as the following:

—Customers pay all our salaries: I must do what it takes to please them.

—Every job in this company is essential and important: I do make a difference.

—Showing up is no accomplishment: I get paid for the value I create.

—The buck stops here: I must accept ownership of problems and get them solved.

—I belong to a team: We fail or we succeed together.

—Nobody knows what tomorrow holds: Constant learning is part of my job.

• Managers change—from supervisors to coaches

When a company reengineers, once complex processes become simpler while once simple jobs grow complex. For instance, the *process* of getting a deal put together at IBM Credit has gone from one that entails four or five different people to one that involves just a single person: A deal structurer does the whole thing. Consequently, the company's managers now have to spend less time keeping the pieces of paper moving through departments but more time helping employees do richer and more demanding work.

Process teams, consisting of one person or many, don't need bosses; they need *coaches*. Teams ask coaches for advice. Coaches help teams solve problems. Coaches are not *in* the action, but close enough to it so they can assist the team in its work.

Traditional bosses design and allocate work. Teams do that for themselves. Traditional bosses supervise, monitor, control, and check work as it moves from one task performer to the next. Teams do that themselves. Traditional bosses have little to do in a reengineered environment. Managers have to switch from supervisory roles to acting as facilitators, as enablers, and as people whose jobs are the development of people and their skills so that those people will be able to perform value-adding processes themselves.

This kind of managing is a real profession. Traditional practice undervalues both work and management. It undervalues work by stating that the only way a worker can get ahead is by becoming a manager. Managing, this implies, is more important than working. But the traditional practice also says that anybody who does well as a worker can manage.

In fact, managing is a particular skill, just like engineering or sales, and there is little correlation between excelling in a work skill and being a good manager. Casey Stengel was an adequate baseball player; he was a great manager. Most great players have made lousy managers.

Managers in a reengineered company need strong interpersonal skills and have to take pride in the accomplishment of others. Such a manager is a mentor, who is there to provide resources, to answer questions, and to look out for the long-term career development of the individual. This is a different role from the one most managers have traditionally played.

- Organizational structures change—from hierarchical to flat

When a whole process becomes the work of a team, process management becomes part of the team's job. Decisions and interdepartmental issues that used to require meetings of managers and managers' managers now get made and resolved by teams during the course of their normal work. Pushing decisions about work down to the people doing it means that managers' traditional roles are diminished. Companies no longer require as much managerial "glue" as they used to in order to hold work together. After reengineering it no longer takes all the king's horses and all the king's men to put fragmented processes back together again. With fewer managers there are fewer management layers.

In the traditional company, organizational structure is an important issue on which enormous amounts of energy are expended. Why? Because organizational structure is the mechanism through which a great many issues get resolved and questions get answered.

Remember that the basic unit of the traditional organization is the functional department, a collection of people performing similar tasks. The organization as a whole consists of these functional departments arranged in various ways. The arrangements vary widely among companies. In the so-called functional company, all related functional departments are aggregated into a single functional division: All sales departments come together in a sales division. In a structure based on strategic business units, functional departments are grouped together by markets, so a company might have an institutional division or a West Coast division, for instance.

A lot of energy goes into designing these organizations because the shape of the organization determines much about it, from how the company's work is organized to the mechanisms for the exercise of control and performance monitoring. The organizational structure establishes the lines of communication within the organization and determines the decision-making hierarchy.

In companies that have reengineered, however, organizational structure isn't such a weighty issue. Work is organized around processes and the teams that perform them. Lines of communication? People communicate with whomever they need. Control is vested in the people performing the process.

Consequently, whatever organizational structure remains after reengineering tends to be flat, as work is performed by teams of essentially coequal people operating with great autonomy and supported by a few managers—few, because while a manager can typically supervise only about seven people, he or she can coach close to thirty. At a one to seven manager-to-worker ratio, an organization is of necessity hierarchical. At one to thirty, it is much less so.

Stephen Israel, a senior vice president at IBM Credit, when asked about his post-reengineering organizational chart, replied, "We have one, but we never look at it." The structure of his organization has become, in a phrase, "A bunch of people doing work." Such a company does not rely on its structure per se to answer many questions. After reengineering the issue of structure is considerably diminished in importance.

• Executives change—from scorekeepers to leaders

Not the least of the changes set off by reengineering is the opportunity and necessity for a shift in the role of a company's senior executives. Flatter organizations move senior executives closer to customers and to the people performing the company's value-adding work. In a reengineered environment, the successful accomplishment of work depends far more on the attitudes and efforts of empowered workers than on the actions of the task-oriented functional managers. Therefore, executives must be leaders who can influence and reinforce employees' values and beliefs by their words and their deeds.

Executives have overall responsibility for reengineered process performance without having direct control over the people performing them. These people are working more or less autonomously with the guidance of their coaches. Executives fulfill their responsibilities by ensuring that processes are designed in such a way that workers can do the job required and are motivated by the company's management systems—the performance measurement and compensation systems—to do it.

In traditional companies executives are divorced from operations. Their perspective on the companies they run is primarily a financial one: Did the company make its numbers this quarter? As leaders in a company that has reengineered, they move closer to the real work. In shaping processes and providing workers with motivation, they're intimately concerned with how the work gets done. No football coach tells the team, "I want you to win by 15 points. Get in there and play, and at the end of the game, report to me how it comes out." Although coaches don't play, they're closely involved in creating the game plan and in the players' performance. So is the executive in a reengineered company. They are far more than just scorekeepers.

Let us summarize the changes that occur when a company reengineers its business processes: Jobs certainly change, as do the people needed to fill them, the relationships those people have with their managers, their career paths, the ways people are measured and compensated, the roles of managers and executives, and even what goes on in workers' heads. In short, reengineering a company's business processes ultimately changes practically *everything*

THE BUSINESS SYSTEM DIAMOND

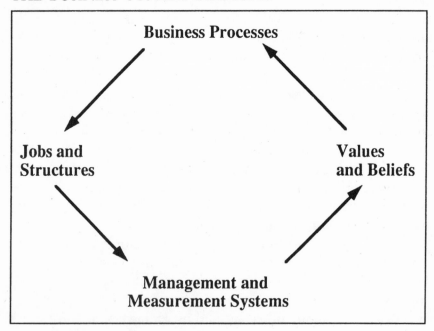

about the company, because all these aspects—people, jobs, managers, and values—are linked together. We call them the four points of the business system diamond. The top point on the diamond is the company's business processes—the way the work gets done; the second is its jobs and structure; the third, its management and measurement systems; and the fourth, its culture—what its employees value and believe.

The linkages are key. The top point of the business system diamond, process, determines the second point, jobs and structure. The ways in which work is performed determine the nature of people's jobs and how the people who perform these jobs are grouped and organized. The fragmented processes found in traditional companies lead to narrowly specialized jobs and organizations based on functional departments. Integrated processes give rise to multidimensional jobs that are best organized into process teams.

Likewise, people who perform multidimensional jobs and who are organized into teams must be recruited, evaluated, and paid by means of appropriate management systems. In other words, jobs and structures, themselves determined by the process designs, in turn lead to the third point on the diamond, the kind of management systems a company must have.

The management systems—how people are paid, the measures by which their performance is evaluated, and so forth—are the primary shapers of employees' values and beliefs, the fourth point on the diamond. By values and beliefs, we mean the issues and concerns that people in the organization think are important and to which they pay significant attention.

Finally, the reigning values and beliefs in an organization must support the performance of its process designs. For example, an order fulfillment process that is designed to operate quickly and accurately will not do so unless the people performing it believe speed and accuracy are important. This brings us back to the top of the diamond. Once again we say that in reengineering it is not sufficient to redesign processes alone. All four points on the business system diamond have to fit together or the company will be flawed and misshapen.

The fact is that every company, even those with traditional organizations, has a business diamond. Reengineering can be thought of as replacing a diamond that has lost its luster and brilliance with a new one.

There is one part of reengineering that we have touched on but not yet discussed. That is the role that information technology plays. It is integral and the next chapter explains why.

CHAPTER 5

THE ENABLING ROLE OF INFORMATION TECHNOLOGY

A company that cannot change the way it thinks about information technology cannot reengineer. A company that equates technology with automation cannot reengineer. A company that looks for problems first and then seeks technology solutions for them cannot reengineer.

Information technology plays a crucial role in business reengineering, but one that is easily miscast. Modern, state of the art information technology is part of any reengineering effort, an *essential enabler* as we termed it in the last chapter, since it *permits* companies to reengineer business processes. But, to paraphrase what is often said about money and government, merely throwing computers at an existing business problem does not cause it to be reengineered. In fact, the *misuse* of technology can block reengineering altogether by reinforcing old ways of thinking and old behavior patterns.

Consider what throwing computers at the problem might have accomplished at the three companies, IBM Credit, Ford, and

Kodak, whose reengineering efforts we examined in Chapter 2.

IBM Credit might have tried to accelerate its tortuously slow turnaround of credit applications by computer-linking the five different species of specialists who processed each one of them. Such a system would have accelerated the old process by eliminating the time required to move pieces of paper from one specialist's office to another. It would have done nothing, however, to eradicate the far greater queue time that awaited the forms when they arrived at each office. By computerizing the process, the company might have achieved a 10 percent performance improvement instead of the more than 90 percent improvement it attained through reengineering.

Ford, too, might have simply computerized its vendor payment process. By doing so, company executives estimated they would have been able to do away with 20 percent of the five hundred jobs in the accounts payable unit. Instead, by reengineering the process, they eliminated 80 percent of those jobs.

Kodak could have shaved a few days from product and tooling design by giving its product and tooling designers state of the art CAD workstations, but it would never have obtained the almost 50 percent reduction in overall product development time that it achieved by reengineering the process.

LEARNING TO THINK INDUCTIVELY

To recognize the power inherent in modern information technology and to visualize its application requires that companies use a form of thinking that businesspeople usually don't learn and with which they may feel uncomfortable. Most executives and managers know how to think *deductively*. That is, they are good at defining a problem or problems, then seeking and evaluating different solutions to it. But applying information technology to business reengineering demands *inductive* thinking—the ability to first recognize a powerful solution and then seek the problems it might solve, problems the company probably doesn't even know that it has.

Ford managers originally thought their problem was to find a method for processing vendor invoices quicker and with fewer people. What they found instead was a solution that let them do away with invoices entirely. IBM Credit's executives thought their problem was how to speed the movement of information among various groups of specialists. Information technology allowed the company to eliminate the specialists, so that it did not need to move the information around at all. Kodak thought its problem was pushing designers to work faster so that succeeding design steps could start sooner. Its technology solution virtually eliminated the need for sequential design.

The fundamental error that most companies commit when they look at technology is to view it through the lens of their existing processes. They ask, "How can we use these new technological capabilities to enhance or streamline or improve what we are already doing?" Instead, they should be asking, "How can we use technology to allow us to do things that we are *not* already doing?" Reengineering, unlike automation, is about innovation. It is about exploiting the latest capabilities of technology to achieve entirely new goals. One of the hardest parts of reengineering lies in recognizing the new, unfamiliar capabilities of technology instead of its familiar ones.

Even Thomas J. Watson, Sr., the founder of IBM, fell victim to this common shortsightedness when he proclaimed that the world-wide demand for data-processing computers would come to fewer than fifty machines. Twenty years later, mainframe computer makers and corporate computer managers both dismissed the minicomputer as a toy. Ten years after that, the personal computer received the same reception: "We're already meeting our needs with large machines," the conventional thinking went, "so why would we need small ones?" The answer, as we can see now, was that the great power of minicomputers, and then of PCs, did not lie in doing what larger machines already did but in giving birth to entirely new classes of applications.

Thinking deductively about technology not only causes people to ignore what is really important about it, it also gets them excited about technologies and applications that are, in fact, trivial and unimportant. Not long ago, for instance, someone thought it would be a terrific idea to integrate the personal computer and the telephone. The integrated unit would save space on desktops and be less expensive than buying separate units. That may be true, but combining the two machines into one doesn't offer any breakthroughs in capability. It doesn't let people do important things that they couldn't do before. It was at best a marginal improvement.

A lack of deductive thinking about technology is not a new problem, nor one confined to laypeople. Early on, many people thought that the greatest potential for the telephone lay in reducing the loneliness of the farmer's wife. Thomas Edison once said he thought the value of the phonograph, which he invented, was its capability to allow "dying gentlemen" to record their last wishes. Marconi, the developer of the radio, viewed it as a wireless telegraph that would operate point-to-point; he didn't recognize its potential as a broadcast medium. The real power of xerography was completely missed by no less a company than IBM.

In the late 1950s, when Xerox was performing the basic research on the 914, its first commercial copying machine, the company was hard pressed for money and wanted to cash out of the project. It offered its patents to IBM, which hired Arthur D. Little (ADL), the Cambridge, Massachusetts-based consulting firm, to do a market research study. ADL concluded that even if the revolutionary machine captured 100 percent of the market for carbon paper, dittograph, and hectograph—the techniques used for copying documents at the time—it still would not repay the investment required to get into the copier business. IBM, on the best evidence available, decided to turn down the Xerox patents and stay out of copiers. Despite the downbeat forecast, Xerox decided to persevere, on the assumption that *someone* would find a use for the machines.

We know now—indeed, it seems obvious—that the power of the Xerox copier did not lie in its capability to replace carbon paper and other existing copying technologies, but in its ability to perform services beyond the reach of these technologies. The 914 created a market for convenience copies that had previously not existed. Thirty copies of an existing document to share with a group of coworkers was not a need people knew they had before the invention of xerography. Since people couldn't make thirty easily and inexpensively, no one articulated doing so as a "need."

What we see operating in these cases of technology creating its own previously undreamed of uses is a variant of Say's Law. Jean Baptiste Say, an early nineteenth-century French economist, observed that in many situations, supply creates its own demand. People do not know they want something until they see that they can have it; then they feel they can't live without it. Alan Kay, often referred to as the father of the personal computer and now Apple Fellow at Apple Computer, puts it this way: "An important technology first creates a problem, and then solves it." No one "needed" the 914 copier—no one knew that they had a problem it solved—until the 914 appeared. Then the latent, unarticulated need suddenly became tangible and overwhelming.

It is, therefore, no use simply asking people how they would use a technology in their business. They will inevitably reply in terms of how that technology might improve a task they do already. One can usefully inquire of people whether they prefer their milk in glass bottles or cardboard cartons. Consumers are familiar with milk and with the two types of containers, and they can provide good information about their preferences and the reasons for them. If, though, a market researcher were to ask people in the pre-xerography days about copy machines, as they did, the respondents would say that it was hardly worth the price just to replace carbon paper.

Similarly, if a market research firm asks a person who travels frequently on business what would make his life easier, he might reply that he would like a faster way to reach the airport, or might express a yearning for a private plane. What he *will not* say he needs is a Star Trek-style teleportation device. He won't, because such a device is outside his frame of reference. When the market researcher mentions business travel to him, the business traveler's mind thinks of the familiar process: Get stuck in traffic on the way to the airport, stand in line, scrunch into seat, eat terrible food. Those are the problems of which he is *aware* and the ones to which he will seek solutions. The true power of technology is to offer answers to problems he does not *know* he has—how, for example, to eliminate air travel completely.

Sony Corporation has achieved a good measure of its success by paying attention to this fundamental precept—that market research done for a product that does not yet exist is useless. When Sony developers first envisioned the Walkman, management did not order up a market research survey to see if the product would be embraced by consumers. Realizing that people are unable to conceptualize what they do not know, Sony gave the Walkman the green light based on developers' insights into people's needs and the capabilities of the technology. The Walkman transformed, rather than responded to, people's ideas about where and how they could listen to music.

The larger point we want to make is that needs, as well as aspirations, are shaped by people's understanding of what is possible. Breakthrough technology makes feasible activities and actions of which people have not yet dreamed. The challenge that most corporations fail to meet is recognizing the business possibilities that lie latent in technology. This shortcoming is understandable if not excusable.

Take, for instance, teleconferencing. This technology allows people located in specially equipped rooms in remote locations to hear and see each other and to work together almost as though they were in the same room. Initially, most organizations saw the value of teleconferencing as a means of reducing travel costs; people would be able to meet without having to fly. In this respect, teleconferencing has, by and large, proved a monumental failure. People travel to be with other people for many reasons. A trip, whether it's across town or across the country, in its very undertaking says something about the importance attached to the message ultimately delivered, of the subject eventually discussed. The nonverbal communication that takes place in a face-to-face meeting is probably more important than most of the words actually spoken. No surprise, then, that teleconferencing has had little effect on corporate travel costs.

That doesn't mean, however, that teleconferencing is without value. It means that its worth lies in transforming how work is done, not in lowering its costs. For instance, one company we know has used teleconferencing to cut its product development cycle by six months. How?

This company's engineering and marketing staffs are based in two different states, so once a month one group would fly to the other's location and, face to face, they would iron out their problems. Now the company has installed teleconferencing facilities, but the engineers and marketers still fly to see one another once a month, because they have found it difficult to resolve all their differences over television. The medium is too cool, and teleconferencing is no substitute for hand-to-hand combat. However, the engineers and marketers do use teleconferencing for weekly discussion sessions, which, previously, they could not hold because of the inconvenience, lost time, and costs associated with travel.

During their weekly teleconferences, the two groups can follow up on the points they discussed at the last face-to-face meeting. Moreover, they can include more people in their discussions. Before teleconferencing, the senior managers were too busy to devote three days—one day to get there, one day to meet, and one day to get home—to a monthly meeting, and it proved too expensive to buy airline tickets for the junior staff involved in the projects. That meant that only the mid-level people met face to face. With teleconferencing, everyone can "meet" once a week, stay informed, and have his or her routine questions answered. As a result, product developers and marketers keep in better touch, problems get resolved earlier and faster, fewer trips get taken down blind alleys, projects are completed faster, and the products they produce are better suited to their markets.

In short, the value of teleconferencing to this company lay in allowing it to do something it had *not* done before: keep marketers and designers in weekly contact. This use had not occurred to the people promoting teleconferencing, because they had not broken out of their old, deductive thinking mode.

To reiterate, the real power of technology is not that it can make the old processes work better, but that it enables organizations to break old rules and create new ways of working—that is, to reengineer.

In building a brand new facility in which to manufacture its Saturn cars, General Motors enjoyed the opportunity to reengineer old work processes without the constraints imposed on it by existing plants. Consequently, GM, which had great ambitions for the Saturn facility, could break rules in a wholesale fashion by capitalizing on the enabling capabilities of information technology.

GM designed the Saturn plant, located in Spring Hill, Tennessee, to include an on-line manufacturing database that is accessible by the company's component suppliers. The suppliers do not wait for GM to send them a purchase order; they simply consult the car maker's production schedule, which is included in the database. Then they take it upon themselves to deliver the appropriate parts to the assembly plant as needed. By knowing how many cars GM plans to make in the following month, for instance, the company supplying Saturn's brakes knows how to configure its own production and shipping schedule. It is the brake manufacturer's responsibility to show up at 8:30 in the morning at the right door at the right plant with the right brakes for the right cars, palletized in line-sequence order. Nobody at Saturn has to instruct the vendor explicitly to do so.

In this process, there is no paper—no purchase order and no invoice. After the parts are shipped, the vendor sends an electronic message to Saturn saying, in effect, "These are the parts we have sent to you." When the box of goods arrive, the receiving clerk scans the bar code printed on it with an electronic wand. The computer can then tell the receiving clerk to what part of the plant the goods should go. The scanning also initiates payment to the vendor.

In essence, information technology—in this case, the production schedule database and electronic data interchange (EDI)—has enabled Saturn and its supplier to operate as one company, to eliminate overhead in both organizations, and to break one of the oldest rules in any corporation's unwritten rule book: Treat vendors as adversaries.

In fact, breaking rules is how we recommend that people learn to think inductively about technology during the reengineering process: Find the long-standing rule or rules that technology allows the company to break, then see what business opportunities are created by breaking those rules. Teleconferencing, for example, breaks the rule that remotely located people can meet only infrequently and at great cost. Now it's possible for those people to meet often and inexpensively in an environment where limitations of geographical separation no longer count.

That insight gives a company a powerful tool for transforming its operations. It is one that can be applied in many areas and to many processes, not just to product development. Several mass merchandisers, such as Wal-Mart and K Mart, are using teleconferencing to allow headquarters-based merchandisers to provide store managers in the field with guidance and advice. Teleconferencing enables them to combine local initiative with centralized expertise.

IBM Credit, Ford, and Kodak used technology to break rules as well. The rules, explicit or not, were neither frivolous nor absurd when they were first articulated. They were expressions of the wisdom people had derived from experience. A smart plant manager runs short of parts only a few times because of unexpected demand before he learns to order a little extra. In the absence of forecasting technology, this practice makes perfect sense. But the advent of that technology breaks the reigning rule about the need for safety stocks to buffer demand.

It is this *disruptive* power of technology, its ability to break the rules that limit how we conduct our work, that makes it critical to companies looking for competitive advantage.

Following are some illustrations of additional rules about the organization of work that can be broken by various information technologies, some of them familiar and some state of the art.

Old rule: Information can appear in only one place at one
   time
Disruptive technology: Shared databases
New rule: Information can appear simultaneously in as many
   places as it is needed

It is sobering to reflect on the extent to which the structure of our
business processes has been dictated by the limitations of the file
folder. When information is captured on paper and stored in a
folder, only one person can use it at a time. Making copies and
distributing them is not always feasible and, in any event, leads to
the creation of multiple and eventually inconsistent versions of the
file. Consequently, work involving this information tends to be
structured sequentially, with one individual completing his or her
tasks, then passing the folder to the next in line.

Database technology changes this rule. It allows many people to
use the information simultaneously.

In an insurance business, for instance, Clerk A can be calculating
an applicant's premium rate while Clerk B checks his or her
credit—both of them using the same application form—since neither job depends upon the other. By allowing one document to
exist in several places at once, database technology can free a
process from the artificial limitations of sequencing.

Old rule: Only experts can perform complex work
Disruptive technology: Expert systems
New rule: A generalist can do the work of an expert

When expert systems technology appeared on companies' radar
screens in the early 1980s, most envisioned its utility in straightforward and simplistic terms: They would exploit it to automate the
work of highly sophisticated experts by capturing their expertise in

computer software. This was an extraordinarily foolish idea for several reasons: The technology is not really up to it; we need to retain the experts anyway, so they can continue to learn and advance in their field; and it is not clear why such clever people would participate in sharing all their knowledge with a computer designed to replace them.

In time, though, more sophisticated organizations have learned that there is more money in not being dumb than in being smart. That is, the real value of expert systems technology lies in its allowing relatively unskilled people to operate at nearly the level of highly trained experts.

A major chemical company, for example, has given each of its customer service representatives an expert system that advises them on product features and relationships. This system has allowed each of them to treat every customer inquiry as a cross-selling opportunity, something that previously only the very best had done.

Generalists supported by integrated systems can do the work of many specialists, and this fact has profound implications for the ways in which we can structure work. As illustrated by the changes at IBM Credit, systems technology allows the introduction of a *case worker*, who can handle all steps in a process from beginning to end. By eliminating the handoffs, delays, and errors inherent in a traditional sequential process, a *case worker*–based process can achieve order-of-magnitude improvements in cycle time, accuracy, and cost.

Old rule: Businesses must choose between centralization and
  decentralization
Disruptive technology: Telecommunications networks
New rule: Businesses can simultaneously reap the benefits of
  centralization and decentralization

Businesspeople "know" that manufacturing plants, service facilities, and sales offices located far from headquarters must be treated as separate, decentralized, autonomous organizations if they are to function effectively and efficiently. Why? Because if every question that cropped up in the field had to be referred back to headquarters for an answer, little would get accomplished—and even that little would be late. Experience teaches that people in the field generally work best if they can make their own decisions.

If companies are relying on old technologies—the U.S. mail, the telephone, or even overnight express—to move their information back and forth, they must sacrifice central management control in order to achieve flexible and responsive field operations.

New technologies, however, free companies from this trade-off. High-bandwidth communications networks allow headquarters to have the same information that field offices have and to see the data that field offices see—and vice versa—in real time. With this shared capability, every field office can effectively be part of headquarters, and headquarters can be part of every field office. That means companies can utilize whatever arrangement—centralization, decentralization, or some combination—best serves their markets.

Information technology enabled Hewlett-Packard, the Palo Alto, California-based designer and manufacturer of instruments and computer systems, to break the time-honored rule that centralization and decentralization are mutually exclusive.

In materials procurement, as in most of its activities, Hewlett-Packard was highly decentralized. It granted its operating divisions virtually complete autonomy in purchasing, because they knew their own needs best. But the virtues of decentralization (flexibility, customization, responsiveness) are purchased at a cost (lack of economies of scale and reduced control). At Hewlett-Packard, decentralized purchasing meant that the company could not take advantage of high-volume discounts available from its vendors. For that reason, Hewlett-Packard estimated that it was spending $50 million to $100 million more each year than necessary on raw materials. Centralizing purchasing would not have "solved" the problem of high cost; it would merely have exchanged it for the twin problems of unresponsiveness and bureaucracy. Instead,

Hewlett-Packard found a third way, through the use of a common purchasing software system.

Under Hewlett-Packard's new approach, each manufacturing division continues to order parts for its division. Now, however, each purchasing unit uses a standard purchasing system. These systems all provide data to a new database, which a corporate procurement unit oversees. Corporate procurement negotiates block contracts and volume discounts with suppliers of selected products on behalf of Hewlett-Packard as a whole. Corporate procurement can do so, because the database gives the unit complete information about the divisions' planned and actual purchases. Once contracts are established, purchasing agents check the database to locate approved suppliers and place orders.

The new process gives Hewlett-Packard the best of centralization—volume discounts—and the best of decentralized buying—meeting local needs locally.

Information technology, used imaginatively, has eliminated the need for separate, fully formed field units with their own overheads, and the banking industry, for one, has already begun to recognize this reality. For years, banks treated branches as P&L centers, but now many banks see a branch only as a point of sale and not as a self-contained organization. The availability of automated teller machines and other high-capacity, real-time data network devices means that branch transactions show up in the central bank's books immediately. Since a branch now becomes just a point of sale, banks can keep people close to the customer without having to relinquish central control of operations.

Old rule: Managers make all decisions

Disruptive technology: Decision support tools (database access, modeling software)

New rule: Decision-making is part of everyone's job

Part of the Industrial Revolution model is the notion of hierarchical decision-making. The worker performing a task is expected only to do the job, not to think or make decisions about it. These prerogatives are reserved for management. These rules were not simply manifestations of industrial feudalism. Managers did in fact have broader perspectives, based on more information, than did lower-level workers. This better information presumably allowed them to make superior decisions.

The costs of hierarchical decision-making, however, are now too high to bear. Referring everything up the ladder means decisions get made too slowly for a fast-paced market. Today, companies say they realize that frontline workers must be empowered to make their own decisions, but empowerment cannot be achieved simply by giving people the authority to make decisions. They need the tools as well.

Modern database technology allows information previously available only to management to be made widely accessible. When accessible data is combined with easy-to-use analysis and modeling tools, frontline workers—when properly trained—suddenly have sophisticated decision-making capabilities. Decisions can be made more quickly and problems resolved as soon as they crop up.

Old rule: Field personnel need offices where they can receive, store, retrieve, and transmit information

Disruptive technology: Wireless data communication and portable computers

New rule: Field personnel can send and receive information wherever they are

---

With wide-band, wireless data communications and portable computers, field people of whatever occupation can request, view, manipulate, use, and transmit data almost anywhere without ever having to run back to the office.

Wireless data communication relies on technology similar to that used in cellular telephones, with the important difference that it allows users to send data instead of, or in addition, to voice. With increasingly miniaturized terminals and computers, people can connect to information sources wherever they are. Otis Elevator's service people, for instance, carry with them small portable terminals. After they repair an elevator, they update the customer's service record on the spot, then send the information via modem to headquarters in Connecticut. Avis has applied the same principle to its rental operations. When a customer returns a car to an Avis lot, an attendant, equipped with a tiny computer, meets the car, pulls up the record of the rental transaction, and enters the charge. The customer never has to visit the office.

Earlier, we noted that high bandwidth communication lets companies break the old rule that says field offices must be autonomous organizations. Wireless data communication goes further and begins to eliminate the need for field offices entirely. Processes such as job progress reporting, insurance claims adjusting, and onsite equipment repair consultation will not depend upon a fieldworker's having to find a phone or a computer terminal. Headquarters can know what the people onsite know when they know it—and vice versa.

Old rule: The best contact with a potential buyer is personal contact

Disruptive technology: Interactive videodisk

New rule: The best contact with a potential buyer is effective contact

---

Some companies have started using interactive videodisks, which allow viewers to watch a video segment on a computer screen and then ask questions or answer them on screen. The initial application of this technology was in training, but the potential power of interactive video far transcends this domain.

Several retailers, for example, are experimenting with interactive video to augment their retail sales force. Customers at these stores can select a product from a menu, watch a video presentation about it, ask questions, then order it with a credit card—all without human intervention. The process may seem cold and impersonal, but customers find it preferable to the usual retail experience: waiting forever for a salesperson only to discover that he or she is uninformed.

Banks have begun using interactive video to explain their increasingly complex services to customers, who can ask the machine to clarify points that they don't understand. Some information is *best* communicated visually—real estate, for instance. Interactive video gives prospective buyers a tour of entire houses—and lets them return to see the master bedroom again if they ask—without their having to leave the broker's office.

Old rule: You have to find out where things are
Disruptive technology: Automatic identification and tracking technology
New rule: Things tell you where they are

Combined with wireless data communication, automatic identification technology lets things—trucks, for instance—tell you constantly where they are. You do not have to look for them, and when you want them to go someplace else, they get the word instantaneously. No more waiting for drivers to hit the next truck stop so they can telephone the dispatcher.

A company that knows in real time where its trucks are, or rail cars or service technicians for that matter, does not need as many of them. It does not require as much redundancy in personnel, equipment, and materials to cover the delays inherent in locating and rerouting things and people in transit.

Some railroads, for instance, are implementing satellite systems to tell them where a given train is at any given moment. The old method of tracking trains involved painting bar-code like symbols on the sides of the rail car. As the train pulled through the station, a machine—in theory, at least—would read the bar code and transmit the train's location to headquarters. We say "in theory" because the system never worked. Not surprisingly, the bar codes became so covered with dust and grime that they were unreadable. With the satellite system in place, the railroad companies will be able to deliver freight cars with the same precision with which overnight carriers deliver packages.

Old rule: Plans get revised periodically
Disruptive technology: High performance computing
New rule: Plans get revised instantaneously

The sheer capacity of increasingly *affordable* computing power creates new application possibilities for companies. Take manufacturing, for instance. Today a manufacturer gathers data on product sales, raw materials price and availability, labor supply, and so on and once a month (or once a week) produces a master production schedule. A computer supplied with real-time data from pointof-sale terminals, commodity markets, and perhaps even weather forecasts, among other information sources, could constantly adjust the schedule to match real-time, not historic, needs.

It should be clear from these examples that further advances in technology will break more rules about how we conduct business. Rules that still appear inviolate today may become obsolete in a year or less.

Consequently, exploiting the potential of technologies to change a company's business processes and move it dramatically ahead of its competitors is not a one-time event. Nor is it something a company can do occasionally, say, once a decade. On the contrary, staying on top of new technology and learning how to recognize and incorporate it into an organization must be an ongoing effort—no different from research and development or marketing. It takes a practiced eye and imaginative mind to spot the potential in a technology that does not at first appear to have any obvious application to a company's work or to see past the obvious to the novel applications of a technology that superficially seems useful only for marginally improving the *status quo*.

Companies need to make technology exploitation one of their core competencies if they are to succeed in a period of ongoing technological change. Those better able to recognize and realize the potentials of new technology will enjoy a continuing and growing advantage over their competitors.

Our view is that if you can buy a technology, it is not new. We subscribe to what might be called the Wayne Gretzky School of Technology. Gretzky, who became the National Hockey League's all-time leading scorer at age twenty-eight, was once asked what made him a great hockey player. He was exceptional, he answered, "because I go where the puck is *going* to be, not where it *is*." The same rule applies to technology. Building a strategy around what one can buy in the market today means that a company will always be playing catch up with competitors who have already anticipated it. These competitors know what they are *going* to do with technology *before* it becomes available, so they will be ready to deploy it when it does become available.

Companies that have had great success with applying technology—American Express, for instance, whose image processing system allows it to send digitized copies of original receipts to both corporate cardholders and their accounting departments and Chrysler with its satellite communications system for helping dealers manage their parts inventories—were asking for the technology they needed well before it appeared on the market. Year after year, Chrysler sent out requests for proposals (RFPs) that outlined what it wanted; when a vendor eventually responded with the needed capabilities, Chrysler was ready to implement. Management knew what rules they wanted to break with the technology before the technology was even at hand.

Companies cannot see or read about a new technology today and deploy it tomorrow. It takes time to study it, to understand its significance, to conceptualize its potential uses, to sell those uses inside the company, and to plan the deployment. An organization that can execute these preliminaries before the technology actually becomes available will inevitably gain a significant lead on its competition—in many cases, three years or more.

It is entirely possible to stay three years ahead of the market on technology. It takes time to move from laboratory to market; there does not exist a technology that will become important in 1996 that is not yet demonstrable today. Smart companies can be figuring out how they will use a technology, even while its developers are still polishing their prototypes.

As an essential enabler in reengineering, modern information technology has an importance to the reengineering process that is difficult to overstate. But companies need to beware of thinking that technology is the only essential element in reengineering.

To reengineer a company is to take a journey from the familiar into the unknown. Reengineering this journey has to begin somewhere and with someone. Where and with whom? That is the question we address in the chapters that follow.

CHAPTER 6

WHO WILL REENGINEER?

Companies don't reengineer processes; people do. Before we delve more deeply into the "what" of the reengineering process, we need to attend to the "who." How companies select and organize the people who actually do the reengineering is key to the success of the endeavor.

We have seen the following roles emerge, either distinctly or in various combinations, during our work with companies that are implementing reengineering.

• *leader*—a senior executive who authorizes and motivates the overall reengineering effort

• *process owner*—a manager with responsibility for a specific process and the reengineering effort focused on it

• *reengineering team*—a group of individuals dedicated to the reengineering of a particular process, who diagnose the existing process and oversee its redesign and implementation

• *steering committee*—a policy-making body of senior managers who develop the organization's overall reengineering strategy and monitor its progress

• *reengineering czar*—an individual responsible for developing reengineering techniques and tools within the company and for achieving synergy across the company's separate reengineering projects

In an ideal world, the relationship among these is as follows: The *leader* appoints the *process owner*, who convenes a *reengineering team* to reengineer the process, with the assistance from the *czar* and under the auspices of the *steering committee*. Let's examine these roles and the people who play them in more detail.

LEADER

The reengineering leader makes reengineering happen. He or she is a senior executive with enough clout to cause an organization to turn itself inside out and upside down and to persuade people to accept the radical disruptions that reengineering brings. Without a leader, an organization can do some "paper studies," can even come up with new process design concepts; but absent a leader, no reengineering will actually happen. Even if it gets started, a leaderless reengineering effort will run out of steam or hit the wall by the time it is ready to implement.

Usually no senior executive is "assigned" the job of leader. It's a self-nominated and self-appointed role. Someone with the clout to carry it off becomes the leader of reengineering when he or she is seized by a passion to reinvent the company, to make the organization the best in the business, finally to get it completely right.

The leader's primary role is to act as visionary and motivator. By fashioning and articulating a vision of the kind of organization that he or she wants to create, the leader invests everyone in the company with a purpose and a sense of mission. The leader must make clear to everyone that reengineering involves a serious effort that will be seen through to its end. From the leader's convictions and enthusiasm, the organization derives the spiritual energy that it needs to embark on a voyage into the unknown.

The leader also kicks off the organization's reengineering

efforts. It is the leader who appoints senior managers as owners of business processes and charges them with achieving breakthroughs in performance. The leader creates the new vision and sets the new standard and, through the owners, induces others to translate that vision into reality.

Leaders must also create an environment conducive to reengineering. Urging people on isn't enough. Any rational person in a corporate environment will react warily, if not cynically, to an executive's insistence that he or she break the rules, defy the received wisdom, and think out of the box. So, while half the leader's job involves urging the process owner and reengineering team to perform, the other half involves supporting them so that they *can* perform. "Be bold," the leader says, "and if you get heat from anyone, pass it on to me. If someone blocks your way, let me know who that person is, and I'll take care of it."

Who fills the leader's role? The role requires someone who has enough authority over all stakeholders in the process(es) that will undergo reengineering to ensure that reengineering *can* happen. This need not be the CEO; in fact, it rarely is. In most large companies, the CEO has concerns that range from raising capital on Wall Street to handling key customers to maintaining peace with the government. Many of these responsibilities direct the CEO's attention outside the company, away from its processes. So, often the role of leader belongs to the chief operating officer or president, whose gaze is directed both outward, toward the customer, and inward, toward the operations of the business.

If a company plans to confine reengineering to just one part of the organization, the leader can occupy a less lofty position. He or she might be the general manager of a division. If that's the case, however, the leader must have authority over the resources involved in performing the division's processes. If, for example, a division uses manufacturing facilities that "belong" to the corporate head of manufacturing, who doesn't report to the division head, then the division head may not have the necessary clout to make changes in manufacturing. So the leader of this reengineering effort would have to reside further up in the hierarchy. For similar reasons, a functional head, such as the vice president of sales or manufacturing, is generally not in a position to play the reengineering leadership role, unless the reengineering effort is completely within the domain of the function.

Leadership isn't just a matter of position, but of character as well. Ambition, restlessness, and intellectual curiosity are the hallmarks of the reengineering leader. A caretaker of the *status quo* will never be able to muster the passion and enthusiasm the effort requires.

The leader must also *be* a leader. We define a leader not as someone who makes other people *do* what he or she wants, but as someone who makes them *want* what he or she wants. A leader doesn't coerce people into change that they resist. A leader articulates a vision and persuades people that they want to become part of it, so that they willingly, even enthusiastically, accept the distress that accompanies its realization.

Moses was a visionary leader. He persuaded the Children of Israel that they should go forward toward a land of milk and honey when all they could see around them was sand. One man couldn't force a whole people to set off into the desert; he had to inspire them with his vision. He also set a personal example. When they arrived at the Red Sea, Moses said, "Here's the plan. We're going to march into the sea, the Lord will part the waters, and we'll walk through on dry land." His followers looked at the Red Sea and said to him, "You first." He went, and they followed. Being out front when the risk presents itself is part of leadership. (This story also demonstrates the value of having your boss on your side, as Moses certainly did.)

The reengineering leader can demonstrate leadership through signals, symbols, and systems.

Signals are the explicit messages that the leader sends to the organization about reengineering: what it means, why we are doing it, how we are going about it, and what it will take. Successful reengineering leaders have learned that they always underestimate how much communicating they must do. Giving a speech or two—or ten—doesn't begin to get the message across. Reengineering is a difficult concept for people to assimilate because it cuts against the grain of everything they've done in their careers. In many cases, they also don't see (or they refuse to see) the need for it. Only someone who is serious about reengineering, perhaps to the point of fanaticism, can send the right signals. Winston Churchill defined a fanatic as someone who can't change his mind and won't change the subject. By that definition, fanaticism is needed in a reengineering leader because constant repetition of the reengineering message is essential if people are to understand it and take it seriously.

Symbols are actions that the leader performs to reinforce the content of the signals, to demonstrate that he or she lives by his or her words. Assigning the company's "best and brightest" to reengineering teams, rejecting design proposals that promise only incremental improvement, and removing managers who block the reengineering effort—over and above their intrinsic value—are important symbolic activities. They prove to the organization that the leader is serious about reengineering.

The leader also needs to use management *systems* to reinforce the reengineering message. These systems must measure and reward people's performance in ways that encourage them to attempt major change. Punishing the innovator when an innovation fails is the best way to ensure that no one ever attempts to be innovative. Progressive Insurance, one of the most successful insurance companies in the United States, thrives on constant innovation. Bruce Marlow, the chief operating officer, expresses his company's approach this way: "We never punish failure. We only punish sloppy execution and the failure to recognize reality."

Management systems should reward people who try good ideas that fail, not punish them. At Motorola, the motto is, "We *celebrate* noble failure." An organization that demands constant perfection discourages people from striving and makes them timid. As Voltaire wrote, "The perfect is the enemy of the good."

Some leaders have found it impossible to begin their reengineering efforts in corporate cultures and organizations that would have proved too resistant to change. Ron Compton, for example, CEO of Aetna Life and Casualty, initiated his reengineering program with a set of actions that seemed to have nothing to do with process redesign. He created a new organizational structure that emphasized the autonomy of major business units and eliminated cross subsidies, installed a new senior management team, and carried out a significant reduction in force that slashed costs and signaled the end of Aetna's traditionally paternalistic culture. None of these steps fits our definition of reengineering, but they helped create an environment in which reengineering could succeed. The power of these changes, says Compton, is that they enabled him to tell the organization that he had "burned his bridges." He had dismantled the old Aetna, so the organization could go nowhere but forward. The German phrase *eine Flucht nach Vorn*, a retreat forward, captures the combination of desperation and ambition that many reengineering leaders find necessary to instill in their organizations.

How much of his or her time should the leader devote to reengineering? After all, a senior business manager has other matters to worry about, including keeping the business alive until the results of reengineering begin to show up. We answer this question in two ways. On reengineering per se, the leader need not spend more than a small percentage of his or her time, typically in performing project reviews and making hortatory speeches supporting the reengineering effort. At the same time, reengineering should so suffuse the leader's consciousness and objectives that it underlies everything that he or she does.

Most reengineering failures stem from breakdowns in leadership. Without strong, aggressive, committed, and knowledgeable leadership, there will be no one to persuade the barons running functional silos within the company to subordinate the interests of their functional areas to those of the processes that cross their boundaries. No one will be able to force changes in compensation and measurement systems, no one will be able to compel the human resources organization to redefine its job rating system. There will be no one to convince the people affected by reengineering that no alternative exists and that the results will be worth the agony of the process.

What if no leader steps forward in the beginning? What if the people first inspired to reengineer aren't positioned high enough in the company's hierarchy to pull it off? Then they must get a leader on board. Doing so will require tact, persistence, and self-effacement. They will have to identify a potential leader, create a sense of urgency in his or her mind, and then introduce the idea of reengineering so that the leader embraces it as his or her own.

We have dwelt on the position of leader because it is so essential to the success of reengineering. Not that the other roles are unimportant, but no other individual involved in reengineering is so key as the leader.

PROCESS OWNER

The process owner, who is responsible for reengineering a specific process, should be a senior-level manager, usually with line responsibility, who carries prestige, credibility, and clout within the company. If the leader's job is to make reengineering happen in the large, then the process owner's job is to make it happen in the small, at the individual process level. It is the process owner's reputation, bonus, and career that are on the line when his or her process is undergoing reengineering.

Most companies lack process owners, because in traditional organizations people do not tend to think in process terms. Responsibility for processes is fragmented across organizational boundaries. That's why identifying the company's major processes is a crucial early step in reengineering. (We will have more to say about how this is done in the next chapter.)

After identifying the processes, the leader designates the owners who will guide those processes through reengineering. Process owners are usually individuals who manage one of the functions involved in the process that will undergo reengineering. To do their reengineering jobs, they have to have the respect of their peers and a stomach for reengineering—they must be people who are comfortable with change, tolerant of ambiguity, and serene in adversity.

An owner's job is not to *do* reengineering but to see that it gets done. The owner must assemble a reengineering team and do whatever is required to enable the team to do its job. He or she obtains the resources that the team requires, runs interference with the bureaucracy, and works to gain the cooperation of other managers whose functional groups are involved in the process.

Process owners also motivate, inspire, and advise their teams. They act as the team's critic, spokesperson, monitor, and liaison. When reengineering team members start to produce ideas that make coworkers in the organization unhappy, process owners shield them from the arrows that others will shoot their way. Process owners take the heat so that their teams can concentrate on making reengineering happen.

The process owner's job will not end when the reengineering project is completed. In a process-oriented company, process, not function or geography, will form the basis of organizational structure, so every process will continue to need an owner to attend to its performance.

REENGINEERING TEAM

The actual work of reengineering—the heavy lifting—is the job of the reengineering team members. These are the people who must produce the ideas and the plans and who are often then asked to turn them into realities. These are the people who actually reinvent the business.

A small point before we dive into who these people are: No team can reengineer more than one process at a time, which means that a company reengineering more than one process will have more than one reengineering team at work. What we are about to say applies to each of them.

Notice, we call these groups "teams," not committees. To function as a team they should be small—between five and ten people. Each team will have two kinds of people on it, insiders and outsiders.

We define insiders as people who currently work inside the process undergoing reengineering. They come from the various functions involved in the process. They know the process, or at least the parts of it that they encounter in their jobs.

But knowing the existing process and how the company currently performs it is a double-edged sword. Intimate knowledge of the existing process will help the team find its flaws and trace the sources of its performance problems. Proximity to the existing process, however, may hamper thinking about the process in new and imaginative ways.

Insiders sometimes confuse what *is* with what *should be*. Consequently, we look for people who have been around long enough to know the ropes but not so long as to think the old process makes sense; they shouldn't have become inured to the illogic of the standard ways of doing things. We also look for mavericks who know the rules but also how to get around them. In general, the insiders assigned to a reengineering team should be the best and the brightest, the company's rising stars.

Next to their knowledge, the most important asset that insiders bring to their reengineering work is their credibility with co-workers. When they say that a new process will work, the people in the organizations from which they've come will believe them. When the time comes to put the new process in place, the insiders will act as key agents in convincing the rest of the organization to buy into the changes.

Insiders by themselves, however, are incapable of reengineering a process. Their individual perspectives may be too narrow, confined to just one part of the process. Further, insiders can hold a vested interest in the existing process and the organization designed to support it. It would be asking too much to expect them, unaided, to overcome their cognitive and institutional biases and to envision radically new ways of working. Left to their own devices, a team made up of insiders will tend to re-create what already exists, with perhaps a 10 percent improvement. They will remain within the frame of the existing process, not break it. To understand what is being changed, the team needs insiders; but to change it, the team needs a disruptive element. These are the outsiders.

Outsiders don't work in the process that's undergoing reengineering, so they bring a higher level of objectivity and a different perspective to the team. Outsiders aren't afraid to ask the emperor about his new clothes; they aren't afraid to ask the naive questions that shatter assumptions and open people's minds to exciting new ways of seeing the world. The outsiders' job on the team is to make waves. Since outsiders are beholden to no one affected by the changes they initiate, they feel more comfortable taking risks.

From where do outsiders come? By definition, they are outside the process, and often, especially in companies that have not reengineered at least once before, they may be from outside the company. Outsiders need to be good listeners and good communicators. They must be big-picture thinkers and quick studies, since they will have to learn a lot in a hurry about each process on which they will work. They need to be imaginative thinkers, capable of envisioning a concept and making it happen.

Companies, in fact, may have many candidates for outsiders inside their organizations. Good places to look are in departments such as engineering, information systems, and marketing, where people with a process orientation and an innovative bent tend to congregate. Companies that don't have appropriate internal outsiders can go outside to find them, typically by engaging consulting firms with track records in reengineering. These consultants bring with them experience that companies may not be able to duplicate on their own.

How many outsiders should serve on the reengineering team? A little contention goes a long way. A ratio of two or three insiders to each outsider is about right.

Insiders and outsiders don't mix easily. As the team members go about their jobs, don't expect sweet reason to rule. Team meetings will more likely resemble sessions of the Russian parliament, which is as it should be. An absence of contention and conflict during reengineering usually signals that nothing productive is happening, but contention and conflict among team members should be directed toward a common end. "Truth," said the Scottish philosopher David Hume, "arises from disagreement amongst friends." To us, friends are people with mutual regard and mutual concern. Team members must be friends who share a common focus: improving the performance of their process. There is no room for private turf and private agendas.

Reengineering teams must be largely self-directed. The process owner is their client, not their boss, and the system that measures and rewards team performance should use as its principal criterion the team's progress toward its target. Moreover, team performance should be the single most important measure of individual member achievement.

To function as a team, members need to work together in one place, which is not as easy as it sounds. It won't happen if the team members remain in the offices they occupied before joining the team. In fact, it won't happen if members stay in offices anywhere. Most companies don't design their facilities with collaborative work in mind. They maintain lots of private or semiprivate rooms designed for solo work and conference rooms for meetings, but they don't have many large spaces suitable for a team to work together in over an extended period of time. This isn't a minor issue; it can prove a serious impediment to a reengineering team's progress. So one job for the leader is to find or commandeer appropriate working space for the team.

Reengineering involves invention and discovery, creativity and synthesis. A reengineering team must feel comfortable with ambiguity. Team members must expect to make mistakes and to learn from them. People not capable of working this way do not belong on the team.

Conventional organizations are analytic and detail-oriented in their problem solving; they place a high premium on finding the right answer the first time. They enshrine what we call the "endless planning, flawless execution" model of problem solving, in which a lengthy period of analysis leads to a plan so perfect that any fool could supposedly carry it out. Reengineering, in contrast, requires the team to go through an iterative learning process as it invents a new way of performing work. Reengineering team members will have to unlearn the traditional problem-solving style, a difficult adjustment for some.

The reengineering team has no official head. Most reengineering teams find it helpful to have a team captain, sometimes appointed by the owner but usually nominated by acclamation by team members. The captain, like George Washington, isn't the king, only *primus inter pares*, first among equals. Sometimes an insider and sometimes an outsider, the captain serves as the team's facilitator and quartermaster. His or her job is to enable team members to do their work. The captain may establish the agenda for team meetings, help the team stick to it, and mediate conflicts. Somebody has to attend to the administrative details, such as scheduling and vacation time, and those tasks are likely to fall to the captain as well. However, the captain's primary role is to act as a team member, just like everyone else.

We are often asked three questions about the reengineering team: How much? How long? What next?

When they ask how much, people want to know what percentage of their time team members should expect to devote to the reengineering effort. We are stringent about this requirement. Parttime assignments don't work. A minimum commitment is 75 percent of each team member's time, for insiders and outsiders alike. A lesser obligation will make it extremely difficult to get anything done. It also risks stretching the reengineering effort out so long that it loses momentum and dies. In fact, we strongly urge that organizations assign team members 100 percent to the team. Besides making it easier for the team members to accomplish what they must, a 100 percent commitment sends a powerful signal to the company that management is serious about reengineering.

The reengineering team is not a ninety-day assignment. Members should remain on the team at least through implementation of the first field pilot site, which usually takes a year, but preferably until the reengineering effort is completed. For insiders, then, joining the reengineering team effectively means leaving existing assignments and home organizations, which is as it should be. Team members should sever old ties, so they can be loyal to the process, to the reengineering endeavor, and to one another. They are not on the team to represent the parochial interests of their former departments, but the company's collective interests. To reinforce this perspective, insiders should not expect to return to their previous jobs when reengineering is over. Rather, they should expect to become part of the new organization that will perform the new process that they are designing. No incentive is quite so effective as the prospect of having to live with the results of one's work.

So far we have discussed what we call the core reengineering team, the group with direct responsibility for the reengineering effort. This core is usually supplemented with an outer ring of part-time and occasional contributors, who make more narrow and specialized contributions to the effort. Process customers and suppliers are often represented on the outer core to make sure that their perspectives and concerns are heard in a direct, unfiltered way. Specialists with expertise in particular disciplines—such as information technology, human resources, or public relations—are often also included in the outer core. They have information that the team needs, and they can be assigned to carry out particular tasks, such as constructing an information system to support the new process or developing a communications plan to describe the new process to the rest of the organization. These individuals' commitments vary, but they are typically involved on an ad hoc basis.

In addition to the leader and the reengineering team, we typically see two other roles emerge as a company reengineers: steering committee and reengineering czar.

STEERING COMMITTEE

The reengineering steering committee is an optional aspect of the reengineering governance structure. Some companies swear by it, and others live without it. The steering committee is a collection of senior managers, usually including but not limited to the process owners, who plan the organization's overall reengineering strategy. The leader should chair this group.

Overarching issues that transcend the scope of individual processes and projects get aired in the steering committee. This group decides, for example, the order of priority among all the competing reengineering projects and how resources should be allocated. Process owners and their teams come to the steering committee for help when they run into problems that they can't resolve on their own. Committee members hear and resolve conflicts among process owners. Part Supreme Court, part mutual aid society, part House of Lords, the steering committee can do much to help an extensive reengineering program succeed.

REENGINEERING CZAR

Process owners and their teams focus on their specific reengineering projects. Who then is concerned with actively managing the reengineering effort as a whole, the aggregate of reengineering efforts across the whole organization? The leader has the right perspective but lacks the time for day-to-day management of the reengineering effort, so he or she requires strong staff support. We call this role the reengineering czar.

The reengineering czar serves as the leader's chief of staff for reengineering. In principle, he or she should report directly to the leader, but we have seen almost every imaginable reporting variation.

The czar has two main functions: one, enabling and supporting each individual process owner and reengineering team; and, two, coordinating all ongoing reengineering activities.

A newly appointed process owner's first call should be to the czar, who knows what needs to get done to make reengineering happen. As keeper of the company's reengineering techniques, the czar should have approaches for accomplishing reengineering that he or she can explain to process owners who are new to the task.

The czar can help select the insiders for the team and can identify—or even provide—appropriate outsiders. The czar will also advise new owners on the issues and problems they are likely to encounter. The czar has been down the reengineering road before, so new travelers won't find it lonesome and frightening.

The czar also keeps a watchful eye on process owners to keep them on track as they proceed through reengineering. The czar may convene and moderate some discussions among the process owners. When the owners of the order fulfillment and material acquisition processes need to coordinate their efforts, the czar should make sure that they do.

The reengineering czar is also concerned with developing the infrastructure for reengineering so that not every reengineering project seems like the first one the company has ever done. Field-tested techniques and a stable of experienced outsiders are two ways in which companies can benefit from their own previous experiences. But there is also a third.

Some elements of an organization's infrastructure, if put in place before the implementation phase of a reengineering project, can smooth and speed the implementation. One such element is information technology. Often, it is possible to anticipate early in a reengineering project (or even before it gets underway) what kind of information systems the organization will need to support the reengineered process. Installing the hardware and supporting software—the platforms—for these systems early will make implementation go much faster. Similarly, if companies learn from early reengineering efforts that reengineered processes demand people who exist only in small numbers in the organization, the company can then recruit more of these people before subsequent reengineering efforts start demanding them, saving time and anguish for the managers of these later projects. There is also much to anticipate in terms of changes in management systems regarding workers' compensation, rewards, and performance measurements. Part of the czar's job is to anticipate these infrastructural needs and to meet them even before they arise.

One final point on the subject of the reengineering czar: We have seen instances when the czar becomes a problem by becoming too controlling and forgetting that the leader and the process owner are in charge. Organizations must guard against this possibility and always remember that the work of reengineering has to be the line manager's job.

These, then, are the toilers in the vineyard of reengineering: the leader, the process owner, the team with its insiders and outsiders, the steering committee, and the czar. In some companies they may have other names or the reengineering roles may be defined differently. That's okay. Reengineering is a young art, and there is room for more than one approach.

From the issue of who reengineers we now turn to the next question: What gets reengineered?

CHAPTER 7

THE HUNT FOR
REENGINEERING OPPORTUNITIES

Processes, not organizations, are the object of reengineering. Companies don't reengineer their sales or manufacturing departments; they reengineer the work that the people in those departments do.

The confusion between organizational units and processes as objects of reengineering arises because departments, divisions, and groups are familiar to people in business, while processes are not; organizational lines are visible, plainly drawn on organization charts, and processes are not; organizational units have names, and processes most often do not.

This chapter illustrates how companies identify their business processes, suggests techniques for selecting the processes that should be reengineered and the order of their reengineering, and stresses the importance of understanding specific processes before attempting to redesign them.

Processes are not something that we invented in order to write about them. Every company on earth consists of processes. Processes are what companies do.

Processes in a company correspond to natural business activities, but they are often fragmented and obscured by the organizational structures. Processes are invisible and unnamed because people think about the individual departments, not about the process with which all of them are involved. Processes also tend to be unmanaged that people are put in charge of the departments or work units, but no one is given the responsibility for getting the whole job—the process—done.

One way to get a better handle on the processes that make up a business is to give them names that express their beginning and end states. These names should imply all the work that gets done between their start and finish. Manufacturing, which sounds like a department name, is better called the procurement-to-shipment process. Some other recurring processes and their state-change names:

Product development: concept to prototype
Sales: prospect to order
Order fulfillment: order to payment
Service: inquiry to resolution

Just as companies have organization charts, they can have process maps that give a picture of how work flows through the company. A process map also creates a vocabulary to help people discuss reengineering.

Figure 7.1 is a high-level process map (slightly simplified) of Texas Instruments' semiconductor business. Four especially interesting characteristics of TI's process map stand out. The first is its simplicity as compared to an organization chart of the same company.

The process map shows only six processes for a $4 billion business. "You know," commented a TI executive about this map, "until we drew this picture we thought we were a lot more complicated than we really are." TI is not unusual in this respect; hardly any company contains more than ten or so principal processes.

At TI's semiconductor division, the main business processes are strategy development, product development, customer design and

Fig. 7.1
TI SEMICONDUCTOR BUSINESS PROCESS MAP

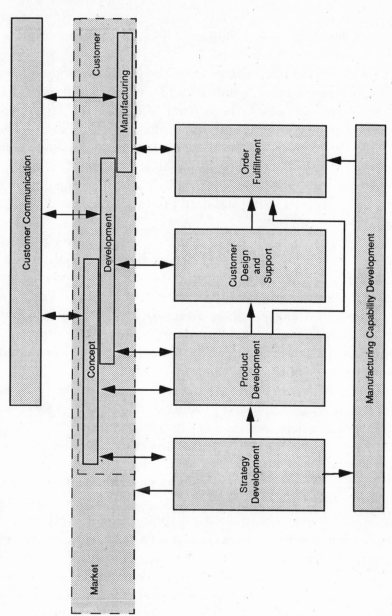

Source: Texas Instruments
(Reprinted with permission)

support, manufacturing capability development, customer communications, and order fulfillment. Each of these processes converts inputs into outputs.

The *strategy development* process converts market requirements into a business strategy, which identifies markets to be served and products and services to be offered. The *product development* process uses this output as input in order to produce new product designs. In some of TI's business lines, general product designs have to be customized for particular customers. The *customer design and support* process creates these so-called "qualified" designs as its outputs, using standard product designs and customer requirements as inputs.

The TI process map shows three other high-level processes. Two of them have names that are probably unfamiliar: *manufacturing capability development* and *customer communications*. The manufacturing capability development process takes a strategy as its input and produces a factory as its output. Customer communications inputs are customer questions and inquiries; its outputs are heightened interest in TI products and consolidated responses to customers.

Order fulfillment is the company's payoff. Order fulfillment converts an order request, a product design, and a factory into a product that is delivered into a customer's hands.

The process map displays a clear and comprehensive picture of the work at Texas Instruments' semiconductor division: Strategy development creates a strategy; product development generates an overall product design; customer design and support produces a custom design; manufacturing capability produces a plant; customer communications answers customer questions and inquiries; order fulfillment delivers what the customer wants.

The second important point to be made about TI's process map is that it includes something that is almost never displayed on a company's organization chart: the customer. On the process map, TI's customer is right in the center.

Point number three is that the TI process map also includes non-customers in its view of processes. These non-customers, who are all potential customers, are included within the "market" label on the map. These non-customers provide important input to the strategy development process.

Fourth, the process map reflects TI's recognition that its customers are companies with processes, too. The customer is not seen as a monolith, but in terms of three key processes with which TI interacts: concept formulation, product development, and manufacturing. This perspective indicates that TI appreciates how its customers' business works and how it can contribute to that work and the customers' processes.

A few processes one might expect to find are not on the map. Manufacturing, for instance. Texas Instruments is a chip maker, but the process portrait does not depict manufacturing as one of its main processes. Instead, manufacturing is a subprocess of order fulfillment—just one of the subprocesses that must get done to deliver a chip to the customer. "Sales" doesn't show up in the picture, either. Sales is not a process, but a department—a collection of people. Salespeople, however, are involved in many of the processes. They're involved in order fulfillment because another subprocess of order fulfillment is order acquisition, which is primarily performed by salespeople. Salespeople will also be involved in the customer communication and in product development processes.

Clearly, then, this map does not represent everything that happens at TI. It shows only the high-level processes. But each of these can explode into various subprocesses—usually numbering no more than half a dozen or so—on separate subprocess maps. Together, the process and subprocess maps give a simple but effective picture of what TI—or any company—does.

Process maps don't require months of work to construct; several weeks is the norm. But this task does induce headaches, because it requires people to think across the organizational grain. It's not a picture of the organization, which is what people are used to seeing and drawing, but a depiction of the work that is being done. When it's finished, the process map should not surprise anyone. In fact, people may wonder why drawing it took as long as it did, since the finished map will be so easy to understand, even obvious. "Of course," people should say, "that's just a model of what we do around here."

CHOOSING THE PROCESSES TO REENGINEER

Once processes are identified and mapped, deciding which ones require reengineering and the order in which they should be tackled is not a trivial part of the reengineering effort. No company can reengineer all its high-level processes simultaneously. Typically, organizations use three criteria to help them make their choices. The first is dysfunction: Which processes are in the deepest trouble? The second is importance: Which processes have the greatest impact on the company's customers? The third is feasibility: Which of the company's processes are at the moment most susceptible to successful redesign?

Broken Processes   In looking for dysfunction, the most obvious processes to consider are those that a company's executives already know are in trouble. As a rule, people are clear about which processes in their companies need reengineering. The evidence is everywhere and generally hard to miss.

A product development process that hasn't hatched a new product in five years can safely be said to be broken. If employees spend time typing data from a computer printout into a computer terminal or from one terminal into another, whatever process they're working on is probably broken. If people's work cubicle walls and their computer screens are papered with Post-it notes reminding them to fix this or look into that, the processes in which they're involved are probably broken too.

Let's look behind some of these symptoms of process distress or dysfunction to the diseases that usually cause them.

Symptom: Extensive information exchange, data redundancy, and rekeying
Disease: Arbitrary fragmentation of a natural process

When employees are keying data taken from one computer into another, it is a symptom of what we call "terminal disease." The efficiency minded manager's typical response to a case of terminal disease is to look for a way to rekey the material more quickly or, if the manager is more technologically oriented, to find a way to link the terminals, so the material can travel electronically from one system to another. Both solutions treat the symptom, not the disease.

When the same information travels back and forth among different organizational groups—whether it's rekeyed each time or transmitted electronically—it suggests that a natural activity has been fragmented. Well-designed natural organizational units should send finished products to one another. Extensive communications is a way of coping with unnatural boundaries. The way to fix the problem is to put the pieces of that activity or process back together. Another name for doing that is cross-functional integration, which allows organizations to capture data just one time and then share it, instead of finding faster ways to ship it back and forth.

Terminal disease doesn't involve only computerized data. If people in different parts of the organization have to telephone one another frequently or send a lot of memos or E-mail messages, that probably means a natural process has been inappropriately broken apart. The typical response to this form of terminal disease is to give the people affected by it more communications links— another phone line, a fancier fax, and so forth. But that treats the symptom not the disease. Indeed, the new devices often fail to treat even the symptom. Our version of Parkinson's Law says that "work expands to fill the amount of *equipment* available for its completion." Give people more communications capacity and they will communicate more and still feel it's not enough.

The fact is—although collaboration may be necessary for some processes—people should not be calling one another *more;* they should be calling one another *less*. To treat the disease, we have to find out why two people need to call one another so often. If what they do is so closely linked, maybe it should be done by one person, a case worker, or by a case team.

Good organizational boundaries should be relatively opaque. In other words, what goes on inside one organizational unit should not be seen or matter very much to people outside it. Organizations should have a thin pipeline connecting them to the rest of the world. If the boundaries of two or more organizations have to be transparent to one another, they probably ought not to be different organizations in the first place.

Symptom: Inventory, buffers, and other assets
Disease: System slack to cope with uncertainty

Many companies are moving to JIT—just-in-time inventory; their current reality in most cases is JIC—just-in-case inventory. Companies, and organizations within companies, know that they will have to supply their output to customers, internal or external. Usually, they're just not certain when the demand will come or how much the customer will need. So they always squirrel just a little extra away somewhere (and sometimes they squirrel away a lot). We are not just referring to just physical assets, either. People create little buffer caches of work, information, cash, and even extra workers against unexpected demand.

The conventional reaction to JIC inventory is to create better inventory management tools. What a company really should work on is getting rid of the inventory. It is there only to take up the slack introduced into the system by uncertainty. Remove the uncertainty, and we have no slack to worry about, so we won't need the inventory.

One way to rid an organization of uncertainty is by structuring processes so that suppliers and customers plan and schedule their respective work together.

Symptom: High ratio of checking and control to value-
adding
Disease: Fragmentation

A lot of work goes on in organizations that does not add value to
the company's product or service. We have a simple test for distin-
guishing work that adds value from work that does not. Take the
customer's perspective and ask, "Do I care?" If the answer is no,
the work adds no value. Does the customer care about a company's
internal controls, audits, management, and reporting? Absolutely
not. That sort of checking and control work doesn't benefit the
customer, only the company. It does not contribute to the value of
the product or the service.

As long as companies consist of people, some amount of checking
and control will be unavoidable. The issue is not whether non-
value-adding work exists in an organization, but whether it forms
too great a portion of all the work the organization performs.

Checking and control work is, of course, a symptom, not the
disease. The root cause—the reason executives and managers think
they must perform checking and control work—is the incompe-
tence and mistrust that can come from fragmentation. The objective
in reengineering is not to make checking and control more efficient,
but to eliminate its root causes.

Symptom: Rework and iteration
Disease: Inadequate feedback along chains

Rework and iteration both involve doing work again that has
been done once—repainting a part that was painted the wrong

color or writing a document several times over. Most often rework and iteration are the consequence of inadequate feedback in a long work process. Problems are not caught when they happen but only much later in the process, requiring more than one step to be redone.

The objective in reengineering is not to get the rework done more efficiently, but to eliminate it entirely by doing away with the mistakes and confusion that necessitate it.

Symptom: Complexity, exceptions, and special cases
Disease: Accretion onto a simple base

When most processes begin life, they are usually quite simple. But they grow complex over time, since every time a new wrinkle or contingency develops, someone modifies the process by adding a special case or a rule to deal with exceptions. Soon the simple process is buried under exceptions and special cases. We may then struggle to simplify what has become unbelievably complicated, but we will fail.

In reengineering we uncover and restore the original, clean process, then create other processes for the other situations. That means we end up with two or more processes instead of just one.

Organizations have become accustomed to standardizing, which means trying to satisfy every contingency with a single process. They create one standard—and complicated—process that has decision points along its entire length. We now know that in process design it is better to install a decision point up front that can send work along one of several simple processes.

The examples listed identify a set of common symptoms or dysfunctions that we often encounter in companies and the diseases, or process problems, to which they are usually connected. But, as we continue to stress, reengineering is as much an art as it is a science, and symptoms don't always point organizational physicians to the correct diagnosis. Sometimes the symptoms can be seriously misleading. In one organization with which we've worked, the order fulfillment processes were badly flawed, but the company's customers didn't think that was the case; they thought the order fulfillment process was superb. They received exactly what they ordered when they wanted it. Superficially, the process appeared healthy. Where did the problem lie? It turned out that the company's sales were limping badly. Was the sales process broken? No. Rather, the order fulfillment process was in such bad condition that customers received their products on time only because salespeople went to the warehouse, picked up the orders, and delivered them themselves. That pleased the customers, but salespeople were making deliveries instead of selling.

In such a situation, we call the slipping sales a secondary sign of dysfunction; a process is broken over here, but the symptoms show up over there. Many times the evidence that a process isn't working exists but it appears somewhere other than in the obvious places. So, while data may indicate that *something* is broken, it may not indicate accurately *which* process isn't working well.

Important Processes Importance, or impact on outside customers, is the second criterion to consider when deciding which of the company's processes to reengineer and in what order. Even processes that deliver their outputs to customers inside the company may be of major importance and value to outside customers. However, companies can't simply ask their customers directly which processes are most important to them, because customers, even if they are familiar with the process terminology, have no reason to know in much detail the processes their suppliers use.

Customers are a good source of information in comparing the relative importance of various processes, however. Companies can determine what issues their customers care strongly about—issues such as product cost, on-time delivery, product features, and so on. These issues then can be correlated with the processes that most influence them as an aid to creating a priority list of those processes that need reconstruction.

Feasible Processes   The third criterion, feasibility, entails considering a set of factors that determine the likelihood that a particular reengineering effort will succeed. One of these factors is scope. Generally, the larger a process—the more organizational units it involves—the broader its scope. A greater payoff is possible when a process larger in scope is reengineered, but the likelihood of its success will be lower. Broad scope means orchestrating more constituencies, affecting more organizations, and involving more managers who have their own agendas.

Similarly, high cost reduces feasibility. A reengineering effort that requires major investment in an information processing system, for example, will encounter more hurdles than one that does not.

The strength of the reengineering team and the commitment of the process owner are also factors to be considered in assessing the feasibility of reengineering a particular process.

We must emphasize that the method used to decide among reengineering opportunities is not a formal one. The three criteria we have outlined—dysfunction, impact, and feasibility—must be used with wisdom to help make choices.

Management might also ask whether a particular business process has a significant effect on the company's strategic direction. Does it have a high impact on customer satisfaction? Is the company's performance in this process far below the best-in-class standard? Is it unable to gain more from this process without reengineering? Is this process antiquated? The more yeses to questions such as these, the stronger the argument for reengineering that process. No two organizations will weigh all of those questions equally. They are, however, the kinds of questions that managers should raise in their search for reengineering opportunities.

UNDERSTANDING PROCESSES

Once a process has been selected for reengineering, a process owner designated, and a team convened, the next step is not redesign—not yet; the reengineering team's next step is to "understand" the current process.

Before a reengineering team can proceed to redesign, it needs to know some things about the existing process: what it does, how well (or poorly) it performs, and the critical issues that govern its performance. Since the team's goal is not to improve the existing process, it does not need to analyze and document the process to expose all of its details. Rather, the team members require a high-level view, just enough so that they have the intuition and insight necessary to create a totally new and superior design.

Nonetheless, one of the most frequently committed errors in reengineering is that at this stage reengineering teams try to analyze a process in agonizing detail rather than attempt to understand it. People are prone to analyze because it is a familiar activity. We know how to do it. It also feels good, because analysis gives us an illusion of progress. We come to the office every morning, and we have calls to make, interviews to perform, data to graph. We produce lots of paper, and it all feels comfortable and satisfying. But analysis doesn't necessarily move us any closer to real understanding.

Detailed process analysis of a conventional sort may be useful to help persuade others in the organization that reengineering is necessary or desirable, but that task is part of change management. What the team is now looking for is knowledge and insight. So, in that the team doesn't have to collect and analyze volumes of quantitative data, understanding a process is less complex and time consuming than analyzing it. However, it is no less difficult. In some ways, understanding is harder than analysis.

Traditional process analysis takes the process inputs and outputs as given and looks purely *inside* the process to measure and examine what goes on. Process understanding, in contrast, takes nothing for granted. A reengineering team attempting to *understand* a process does not accept the existing output as a given. Part of understanding a process is comprehending what the process's customer does with that output.

The best place for the reengineering team to begin to understand a process is on the customer end. What are the customers' real requirements? What do they say they want and what do they really need, if the two are different? What problems do they have? What processes do they perform with the output? Since the eventual goal of redesigning a process is to create one that better meets customer needs, it is critical that the team truly understands these needs. Understanding customer needs doesn't mean asking customers what those needs are. They'll say only what they *think* they want.

For example, in the case we discussed earlier involving Wal-Mart and Procter & Gamble, P&G might simply have asked Wal-Mart, "What would you like our invoices to look like?" Or, "Do you want the goods delivered faster?" But that is not what happened.

Instead, P&G and Wal-Mart together stepped back and asked, "What is Wal-Mart's real challenge?" The answer in this case was maximizing its profits from selling diapers. Then P&G could ask, "How can we help you sell diapers more profitably? What problems do you have? What do you need?" This is very different from, "How can we help you improve the quality of the existing interaction between us?" Understanding means considering the customer's underlying goals and problems, not just the mechanics of the process that links the two organizations together.

This understanding cannot be obtained merely by asking customers what they want, since they will tend to answer from their own unexpanded mindset. They'll say they want it—whatever "it" they already get—a little faster, a little better, a little less expensively. Customers, when asked, will respond with not very surprising ideas for making incremental improvements to the existing process. That is not what a reengineering team is after.

Rather, a reengineering team has to understand the customers better than they understand themselves. Toward that end, the team, or some of its members, might move in and observe and/or actually work with customers in their own environments. Doing this is another way in which gaining understanding differs from analysis. In traditional analysis, people collect information through interviews that take place in offices or conference rooms. They don't interview at real work sites, because it is considered much too noisy and distracting there. So, analysts take people out of their work environment, sit them down, and ask them to explain what they do. What people tell analysts, however, is what they *think* they should be doing, what they happen to remember, or what they've been told to say; they do *not* tell what they actually do. What people do and what they say they do are almost never the same.

A better way to acquire information about what customers do is to *watch* them do it. A still better way is for team members to do it themselves. Neither observation nor participation will make experts out of team members after a few days or weeks, but they will come away from the experience with a better idea of what is important and what is not than they would from any interview.

Being there, not just hearing about being there, can help team members see beyond the customers' blinders as well as their own biases. The point is not to learn how to do the customers' work but to understand their business—and to gather ideas.

Ideas will spring from team members seeing and comprehending how the customer uses the output of the process. If, for example, the customer has to partially disassemble the output before using it, maybe the output should be shipped in a partially assembled state. The team is looking for ideas about ways the process can better serve the customer.

Once the team understands what the process customer might need, the next step is to figure out what the process currently provides—to understand the current process itself.

The goal is to understand the what and the why, not the how, of the process, because in redesign the team is less concerned with how the process works today than in what the new process will have to do. Knowing what and why, the team can begin its redesign with a blank sheet of paper. To learn the what and why, the reengineering team can take almost all of what we have just said about observing, and participating in, customers' work and apply those same remarks to the process itself. Observing and performing the process is the best way to develop insight into it. However, the team must be vigilant about avoiding the temptation to overstudy. The goal must be to move quickly to redesign.

Before concluding we should comment on another tool that is available to reengineering teams, namely benchmarking. Essentially, benchmarking means looking for the companies that are doing something best and learning how they do it in order to emulate them.

The problem with benchmarking is it can restrict the reengineering team's thinking to the framework of what is already being done in its company's own industry. By aspiring only to be as good as the best in its industry, the team sets a cap on its own ambitions. Used this way, benchmarking is just a tool for catching up, not for jumping way ahead.

Benchmarking can, however, spark ideas in the team— especially if teams use as their benchmarks companies from outside their own industries. For example, the idea around which Hewlett-Packard reengineered its materials purchasing process came from a senior manager who joined the company from the automotive industry. He brought with him a completely different mindset—and a new purchasing model.

If a team is going to benchmark, it should benchmark from the best in the world, not the best in its industry. If a team's company is in the consumer packaged goods business, the question is not who is the product developer in packaged goods, but who is the best product developer—period. That's the company from which the team might get great ideas.

There's an old story that when Xerox decided to improve its order fulfillment process, it didn't compare itself to other copier companies, but to the mail-order clothing retailer, L.L. Bean.

There's still a danger, however, even in using benchmarking to generate new ideas. What if it doesn't turn up a new idea? It is possible that no one in another company has had a great idea yet that is applicable to the process that the team is seeking to reengineer. Just because that's the case, however, doesn't give the reengineering team an excuse to be complacent. Rather, team members might consider it a challenge: *They* can create the new, world-class benchmark.

Keep in mind that by diagnosing the company's current processes, the reengineering team is learning a great deal about them, but not so that it can fix them. Old processes can take only so much fixing before the marginal benefits aren't worth the bother. Besides, reengineering teams don't look for marginal benefits, but order-of-magnitude improvements. Just fixing the old processes is not enough.

Instead, the team is trying to study the existing processes so it can learn and understand what is critical in their performance. The more team members know about the real objectives of a process, the better they will be at its redesign.

THE EXPERIENCE OF PROCESS REDESIGN

For a writer, nothing is so exciting and at the same time so terrifying as a clean sheet of paper or a blank computer screen. For a reengineering team, it's the first redesign session. All the team has to do in this session is to get a start on reenvisioning the company and inventing a new way of doing its work.

Redesign is the most nakedly creative part of the entire reengineering process. More than any other, it demands imagination, inductive thinking, and a touch of craziness. In redesigning processes, the reengineering team abandons the familiar and seeks the outrageous. Redesign asks the team members, especially the insiders, to suspend their belief in the rules, procedures, and values that they've honored their whole working lives. Redesign is unnerving precisely because the team can do whatever it likes.

The bad news about redesigning a work process is that it is not algorithmic and routine. There are no seven- or ten-step procedures that will mechanically produce a radical new process design.

The good news about redesign is that while it may require

creativity, it's not necessary to start with an entirely blank slate. Enough companies have now done reengineering for us to be able to discern some recurring patterns in the processes they have redesigned. Techniques that have proved effective for some companies will work for others—or at least pieces of them will. So, while no hard and fast rules yet exist for process redesign, we do know the principles on which redesign depends, and we now have some precedents.

Almost anyone who has been through business school or who has a few years of corporate management experience can design a traditional business process, because well-established guidelines exist for doing that. For instance, we know, almost intuitively, that in a traditional process work should be broken into simple tasks; we know the limits of a manager's span of control; we know about economies of scale and the need for control, accountability, and budgeting. Given a business activity—paying vendors for received materials, for instance—almost anyone who has been around a business could design a traditional process for accomplishing it.

It turns out that nontraditional processes also contain recurring characteristics and themes. Not many people know what these are yet, but they are reflections of the principles of reengineering that we have been discussing throughout this book.

Some day the characteristics of reengineered business processes will undoubtedly be as obvious and as well known as the traditional business processes are today. The reason that these nontraditional characteristics and themes are not intuitively obvious to most people today is that they are still new. They have not yet become part of the collective conventional wisdom.

So, how does a reengineering team proceed with its redesign effort? It's the first morning of the redesign phase. The team members are in their meeting room, the coffee is fresh, and the chalkboard is blank. Where to begin?

Process redesign should be breathtaking on account of its potential effects on the company, but it needn't be intimidating. We've developed some techniques that teams can use to get themselves started, and we have some ideas about how to keep people's creative juices flowing during redesign.

In this chapter, we're going to handle redesign in two ways. First, we'll take readers through a short scenario that illustrates how the first day of a redesign session might go. Our objective here is to give people a feel for the redesign process and to show that it need not be mysterious or daunting. Then we'll introduce and illustrate some of the techniques and devices that reengineering teams have found to be useful aids in process redesign.

THE REDESIGN SESSION

Scene: A meeting of the reengineering team at Imperial Insurance, a fictitious but representative auto insurance company. The team's charter is to redesign the accident claims process for Imperial, whose claims payout has soared in recent years. Imagine that this is the team's first redesign session and that you are an outsider sitting in. All you know about the insurance business is what the average person knows and a few things that the team captain covers before the redesign session begins.

First, the captain says, Imperial believes that it is paying out more than it should in settling auto accident claims. The claims typically involve two kinds of payments—one covering injury to people and the other covering damage to automobiles. Settlements on both kinds of claims are rising rapidly.

With medical costs in general growing more expensive, it is not surprising, the leader says, that medical claims settlements are becoming costlier, but the increase in auto damage claims, on the other hand, is a paradox. Some years ago, consumers began buying policies with higher collision deductibles, and the assumption in the industry then was that collision damage claims would go down. But they didn't. They went up. Customers, it now seems, buy the higher deductible policies to cut their premium costs, but after an accident they try to get the company to pay the full cost of repair anyhow. They persuade the body shop to make its estimate high enough to cover the actual repair cost plus some or all of the deductible.

Second, the captain says, Imperial has internal cost problems, too. For every $7 it pays out to settle a claim, the company spends $1 just to process the claim. Furthermore, the company requires an average of forty days to settle a claim, and that's if the claimant doesn't choose to litigate.

He then describes, in a nutshell, Imperial's claims settlement process. When an accident occurs, the claimant first calls his or her agent, who then notifies the company. It can take three days for the company to receive notification by phone, mail, or in person; to enter the notification into the computer; and to get a representative assigned who is qualified to handle the claim.

Once a rep is assigned to the case, his or her first task is to verify that the claimant's policy was current at the time of the accident. If not, the process ends there. If the policy was current, the process continues.

The next series of tasks boils down to getting answers to two basic questions. Whose insurance company is going to pay, and what is it going to cost to settle this claim?

To ascertain costs, the rep discusses the injuries and their treatment with doctors and the injured parties and sets up an appraisal to estimate the cost of repair to the cars. A lot of telephone work is involved here.

To determine who is at fault, the rep schedules interviews with the insured, any other claimants, witnesses, and the police; the rep will also probably make multiple visits to these people and to the accident scene.

Many variables affect the determination of both the repair and the medical costs: How much fixing do the cars really need? Do we have to use factory-made replacement parts or can we use after-market parts? How much medical treatment is enough medical treatment?

None of these questions is easily answered, and it typically takes a rep thirty-five days from the time of the accident to gather enough information to decide whether to offer the claimants a settlement and, if so, to decide how much to offer.

If everyone accepts the settlement offered, the process ends, having stretched out, on average, more than forty days. If any claimant decides to litigate, however, the process can drag on forever. It is not uncommon for litigation to take five years.

For all claims against it, Imperial's average settlement, according to the team captain, comes to $3,500. The internal cost of reaching that settlement runs, on average, $500.

And that's about all you and the team know about Imperial's claims settlement process (which is typical for the industry). The reengineering team's assignment is to redesign the process so that Imperial's auto insurance business becomes profitable. Team members look at one another and the blank yellow pads in front of them. Where to begin?

"Separate those with bodily injury from those without," suggests a team member. "Our biggest exposure comes when there's bodily injury."

"So, why not triage by exposure?" says your neighbor. "Large exposure, small exposure. Sometimes, there can be little or no bodily injury but lots of potential property damage."

"Okay," says the team captain, "we could triage by exposure— small and large. Small exposure would be what? Let's say, no bodily injury and minor damage. Large exposure would be everything else. If we did that, then what? How do we handle the two kinds of claims differently?"

"Well," says a woman across the table, "right now, with overhead and so on it costs us about as much per hour to work on a small claim as on a large one, so I'd say we should try to get the small ones settled fast. They're not worth spending much time on."

"What if we didn't handle them at all?" asks a man at the end of the table. "What if we just paid them, whatever they were, so long as they were smaller than some amount?"

"I don't know," says the captain. "What if we did do that?"

"We have to do *something*," says the woman across from you.

"Let the agent do it," says the man at the end. "If the claim is less than some amount, just let the agent handle it. The agent can pay it. That way it gets done fast, the agent cements his or her client relationship, and we don't invest any time at all in it."

The captain is taking notes on the chalkboard when the man on your left pipes up: "Let the body shop handle it."

Everyone looks at him. Body shops are not traditionally the insurance company's friend.

"How interesting," the captain finally responds after a few seconds' pause. "Let the body shop handle it."

"Yeah," the man says. "They're the ones that determine the price of repair anyway. Maybe there's a way to get them working *for* us instead of being in cahoots with clients that are trying to rip us off."

A crazy idea? Maybe not. Currently when auto body damage is involved, Imperial sends out an appraiser who looks at the cars and determines an appropriate cost of repair. Meanwhile, the customer is getting his or her own estimates, so the company often ends up arguing with its client over the cost of repair. Who is happy in the end? Usually no one.

A man from the sales side of the business says he doesn't think the idea is crazy. "What do we give the customer now?" he asks. "A check. But what does the customer really want? A repaired car. What if we could triage these claims and if there was no bodily injury and only minor damage then we tell the client, just take the car to this auto body shop and they'll take care of it—or, better, tell the customer, here's a list of approved body shops. Pick the one most convenient to you, and they'll take care of it."

Naturally, someone asks what he'd do about fraud—body shops that pad their bills or customers who make claims for accidents that never occurred—and a long discussion follows. The gist of the idea that emerges is this: First, the company could designate preferred provider body shops that would value the steady business and want to keep it. They would cooperate with Imperial in periodic statistical monitoring of the pricing and the quality of their repairs. As for the dishonest customer, Imperial could make claim frequency part of the triage process.

"So," the captain sums up, "here's an idea that we think might work. We set up a triage system. We get a claim for an accident involving no bodily injury and only moderate damage. It comes from a customer who hasn't made a claim in ten years. We can therefore assume that it's not fraud. There's no large exposure. And we are pretty sure the body shop isn't going to rip us off, because we'll be running a statistical audit. So, we send the customer a list of approved body shops and pay the bill when it comes in. That's pretty straightforward, it cuts out a lot of administrative expense, and we can get the claim settled in a lot less time."

He writes on the chalkboard for a minute and then asks the group whether there isn't something more they could do with this notion—settling claims fast.

In traditional insurance claims processes, time has always been considered important. Most claims operations tended to think the *slower* they paid the better, because the company could hold on to the money longer and collect more investment income on it.

"Why might we want to speed it up?" the captain asks and looks around at the group. There's a man sitting next to you on the other side who hasn't said anything yet.

"I'll tell you why," he says, "because it might help keep the client away from personal injury lawyers." In the auto insurance industry as a whole, statistics show that when an attorney is involved the payout to the customer is many times greater than when there is no attorney.

"When are customers most likely to call an attorney?" the man asks rhetorically. "Right at the beginning. You're in an auto accident. You call your agent. You're stressed, angry, unhappy. The agent takes down a lot of information, and then what happens? Nothing, not a damn thing. We spend the next week or so passing paper back and forth, and as far as the claimant is concerned, no one is doing anything for her or him. No wonder they start calling their lawyers."

"What actually happens during those first few days," the captain reminded the rest of the team, "is that reports sit around in in-baskets. We have to find the right rep, who may be on vacation or on the road with another case. Something is happening, but not so the client notices, and we also incur extra claims costs as a result. So, if we want to speed this process up, what should we do?'

Someone suggests an 800 number, well publicized, that customers could call. Someone suggests having accident investigation teams in the office, on call, twenty-four hours a day. Someone suggests giving clients cellular phones so they could call from their cars. Someone suggests installing alarms in car airbags that would call the company automatically if the air bag deployed in an accident. Someone suggests tying in to the police communication system for reporting accidents.

"Good, good, good," the captain says, taking notes on the board. "The idea here to get rapid notification of the accident. Let's review what we have from the beginning. Through one mechanism or another we compress the time required to start the claims process. We get early notification. We check the coverage, we get some basic data about the event, and then we do triage. Easy case? Let the agent pay it off or send the car to one of our preferred provider body shops to take care of it. What about the other cases, though, the ones we can't get rid of quickly? Are there some rules that need to be broken here? Anybody?"

"I don't know much about insurance," you say (the first time you've spoken up in this redesign meeting), "but from what I've heard there seems to be a rule that I think needs to be broken. It's the one that says that the company won't do much for the claimant until it decides who's at fault. From a customer's point of view, I think the rule ought to be fix it first and decide whose fault it is later."

"That's a good statement of a rule that could be broken," the captain tells you. "What if we just eliminated the rule? Maybe we don't need a rule about what we do first. We go to work right away on both fronts—getting things fixed and finding fault. We don't wait to pay until we've found fault."

"Wait, wait," cries another reengineering team member, who has problems with the idea of paying out money that the company might not owe. Another long discussion ensues. The group decides that the company might easily pay money that it didn't owe, but in most cases it would recover that amount from the other insurance company. Plus, its total payout would still be smaller, people feel, if speedy action reduces the number of lawsuits filed against it.

"What else do we need to do here?" the captain asks. "What's the problem from the claimant's point of view? Our visitor (you) raised this point."

"No contact," someone responds.

"Meaning what?"

"We may be working, but the claimant still thinks nothing is going on."

"Suppose you're a claimant," the captain suggests. "You're in the hospital. Your back hurts. You don't know about your car. How do you feel? Terrible. What should we do?"

"Send someone to hold your hand," a team member says.

"Right," says another. "More generally, we've got to get away from the idea that our whole role is to issue a check. Our goal has to change. Instead of issuing checks it should be keeping claimants happy."

"How do we do that?" the captain asks.

"Solve their problems," the last man says.

"How?"

Lots of talk ensues now about what the claimants' problems are and how they get solved. What the company does currently, for instance, is allow clients whose cars are wrecked to rent replacements pending repairs. But, the group decides, that's not solving the customer's problem. That's letting the customer solve his or her own problem, with us just paying for it afterward. Anyway, it's expensive. The claimant pays retail for a rental car. We could strike a better deal with the rental agency.

At this point, the team decides to give the claimants names to make discussion easier. Joe is insured by Imperial and his car is damaged. Sally is the other driver, and she is insured by another company. Not only is her car a total loss, she is in the hospital with neck and back injuries.

"So here's what we do," says a team member. "Sally calls up and says his car is totaled. We say, 'Oh, no, that's terrible. We'll have a replacement car at your house in an hour.' Is Joe happy? Thrilled. And we're saving money, because we're going to deliver Joe a mid-sized car, not the Lincoln he might have rented, and we're going to pay only $10 a day for it, not the $30 a day it would have cost him."

Nor does the team forget about Sally. Imperial isn't her insurer, but at this point who knows who's going to have to pay? What does the company want to be to Sally at this point? Warm, the group decides—a friend. Sally needs to see a kind and sympathetic person from Imperial in her hospital room. The explicit message will be, we're here to help. The implicit message? Don't sue. Also, maybe if we provide Sally such good service, she will switch to us. So claims processing becomes a sales opportunity.

One thing that customers like, someone says, is not having to deal with lots of different people on a claim. "What if we could make it so they had to deal with only one person?" "Okay, what if we did?" responds the captain. The team discusses creating something they call a case manager. Sally's in the hospital, and she's concerned about her car. The case manager will take care of it for her.

Sally has a bunch of different doctors, but none of them is going to solve her nonmedical problems. The case manager can. And by being on top of the situation, the team captain points out, the case manager can make sure that Sally gets good but not unnecessary medical care, which means that the company saves money again.

That's as far as the reengineering team got in its first redesign session. The team members haven't finished by any means. They still have lots of numbers to analyze and details to check, but they did get a good day's work done. They got over the first big hump, which is the challenge of coming up with big ideas. They didn't get mired in the old conventions. They were able to color outside the lines, to think outside of the box. And the team captain was good at provoking team members to speak up with ideas that might have seemed on their face absurd—the idea, for instance, of letting body shops settle small repair claims for clients without company investigation and appraisals. "How interesting," the captain said, inviting other team members to carry the idea even further.

In that instance, the team members were employing a technique that we often find useful. They were carrying a principle of reengineering—one that says work is best organized around outcomes, not tasks—to its logical extreme just to see where it leads. As a result they got a good idea, the one involving body shops.

Let's examine how the team might have applied another reengineering principle to guide them in their effort. The one we show here is by no means the only principle we might use; indeed, the ongoing discovery and articulation of the principles underlying reengineered processes is one of our major continuing efforts. Nonetheless, the following illustrates how applying new design principles can spark powerful ideas.

Principle: As few people as possible should be involved in the performance of a process.

Not all redesigned work processes end up in the hands of a single worker, but that isn't a bad goal for which to strive. Imagine that only one person were available to handle an insurance claim. What tasks would have to be eliminated or combined to make that possible? What work would have to be shifted outside—to, for instance, the body shop? Had the reengineering team at Imperial Insurance applied this one worker assumption, it could have triggered the idea of a case manager. More generally, imagine that only a single person were available to perform all the tasks involved in building a product. How would he or she be likely to do it? What help would that single worker need? How could technology lend a hand? These are the kinds of questions that will generate big ideas.

Asking themselves questions based on this and other principles of reengineering and seeing where the answers lead them is one technique that reengineering team members can use to get the redesign process moving. The objective of raising such questions is not to produce final answers but to stimulate the group's creative juices.

Another technique that we often find useful in stimulating the reengineering team members' thinking is that of identifying and annihilating assumptions.

Assumptions are deeply held beliefs that underlie and are built into almost every existing business process. If for instance, field salespeople are not allowed to set the terms of the deal, it is a consequence of the assumption that salespeople put their own financial interests ahead of the company's in order to get a commission. The practice of paying suppliers only after receiving their invoices is based on an assumption that it would be impossible to correlate received goods directly with purchase orders. If a company maintains regional distribution centers, it may be because it assumes that regional centers provide better service than a centralized distribution operation.

A reengineering team can try turning these assumptions on their heads or throwing them out entirely and see where that leaves the process they are redesigning.

The Imperial Insurance team implicitly questioned the assumption that all body shops overcharge to see what steps or tasks in the process that might allow them to eliminate. They also determined what needed to be done to make the assumption invalid (in this case, it was the periodic monitoring of body shop performance).

The Imperial team also questioned the assumption that fault had to be determined before anyone could get paid. The result was a streamlined and faster process.

One of the t-shirt slogans of the sixties read, "Question authority." Process owners might buy their reengineering team members the nineties version: "Question assumptions."

A third technique that reengineering teams can use to stimulate their own creativity is to harness the disruptive power of information technology.

As we stressed in Chapter 5, conventional business process structures reflect the limitations of the pre-computer era technologies on which the designs of these processes were based. The limitations of those technologies—the number of carbon copies a typist could produce or the amount of information one could send between headquarters and field offices through the mail or over the telephone—are deeply embedded in existing processes. When we try to improve these processes, we are still too often constrained by these same limitations.

Reengineering teams can break out of this bind by starting with the capabilities of modern information technology. See what technology allows you to do, and then determine if this helps you rethink the process.

For example, on-line computer databases allow Imperial to check easily on the claims-filing history of any particular customer and on the nature and cost of the repairs for which the company has paid various auto repair shops. With that never-before-available capability in mind, Imperial's reengineering team could reshape the damage-appraisal process, which was time-consuming, expensive, and damaging to the company's relationships with its claimant customers.

We have mentioned three kinds of techniques that reengineering teams can use to help them get the ideas flowing: One, boldly apply one or more principles of reengineering; two, search out and destroy assumptions; and three, go looking for opportunities for the creative application of technology. As redesign proceeds, teams can come back to these techniques to stimulate additional thought or get themselves over a hump.

Although Imperial Insurance is a fictitious company, the ideas we mentioned in the discussion are all plausible. Everything the Imperial reengineering team thought of is currently under consideration or implementation at a real insurance company.

Beyond the specific techniques noted above, the Imperial case teaches other important lessons about reengineering. In seminars, we often ask participants to play the roles of the Imperial reengineering team members. Afterwards, we ask them to reflect on the experience that they have just had and tell us what else, besides the three techniques, they have learned about the experience of redesign. It's uncanny how often we get the same eight answers. Here's what the role-players usually say they have discovered:

1. You don't need to be an expert to redesign a process.
2. Being an outsider helps.

3. You have to discard preconceived notions.
4. It's important to see things through the customer's eyes.
5. Redesign is best done in teams.
6. You don't need to know much about the current process.
7. It's not hard to have great ideas.
8. Redesign can be fun.

Redesign can be fun, but eventually comes the sobering moment when the reengineering team has to explain what it's been doing to the rest of the company—to the people who will have to adjust to and live with the team's redesigned processes. The team has to move from having ideas to making them happen. That part of the reengineering process can be less fun.

CHAPTER 9

EMBARKING ON REENGINEERING

We have held off until now to discuss a crucial aspect of reengineering, one that actually has to begin at the very outset of the effort. The reason we have waited until this point, by which readers have acquired a grasp of the power and immensity of reengineering as a tool for reinventing companies, is that otherwise the significance of this deferred topic would have been easy to miss. What we are now discussing is the tremendous challenge of persuading the people within an organization to embrace—or at least not to fight—the prospect of major change.

Getting people to accept the idea that their work lives—their jobs—will undergo radical change is not a war won in a single battle. It is an educational and communications campaign that runs from reengineering's start to its finish. It is a selling job that begins with the realization that reengineering is required and doesn't wind down until well after the redesigned processes have been put into place.

In our experience, the companies that have the most success in selling change to their employees are those that have developed the clearest messages about the need for reengineering. Senior managers in these companies have done the best job of formulating, and articulating two key messages that they must communicate to the people who work in their organizations. The first of these is: Here is where we are as a company and this is why we can't stay here. The second is: This is what we as a company need to become.

The first message must make a compelling argument for change. It must convey a forceful message that reengineering is essential to the company's survival. This is a crucial requirement because employees who aren't convinced of the need for change will be disinclined to tolerate it and may even obstruct it. The process of developing this argument has the additional benefit of forcing management to look honestly at the company and its performance in the context of a broad competitive environment.

The second message, what the company needs to become, gives employees a palpable goal for which to shoot. Articulating it forces management to think clearly about the purpose of their change program and about the extent of the change that needs to be effected through reengineering.

We have names for the documents that companies typically use to articulate and communicate these two essential messages. We call the first a "case for action" and the second a "vision statement." The names themselves are not important—various companies have given them different names—but the contents matter a great deal.

The case for action says *why* the company must reengineer. It has to be concise, comprehensible, and compelling. It can't just be management crying "Wolf!" It has to be a *case* for action—a dramatically persuasive argument, supported by evidence, that spells out the cost of doing anything short of reengineering. If a company stands to lose its competitive advantage in a particular line of business, the case for action should say so. If the company is seeing a steady erosion of its profit margins, the case for action should show that. If a company faces outright failure, the case for action should argue that, too—but only if it is true. The document must present a strong case, but it cannot exaggerate. The case for action must be so persuasive that no one in the organization will think that there is any alternative to reengineering. Most of the facts in the case for action probably won't be newly discovered, but by capturing them in a single document, the case for action makes people see that the organization is indeed broken.

The case for action should be brief—five to ten pages at most—and blunt. We admire the one that follows, which senior managers of a major pharmaceutical company prepared to convince their employees that the organization's research and development process had to be radically altered. This case for action contains all the elements we think are important, and it presents them economically.

CASE FOR ACTION
PHARMACEUTICAL COMPANY

• We are disappointed by the length of time we require to develop and register new drugs in the United States and in major international markets.

• Our leading competitors achieve significantly shorter development cycles because they've established larger-scale, highly flexible, globally integrated R&D organizations that operate with a uniform set of work practices and information systems.

• The competitive trend goes against our family of smaller, independent R&D organizations, which are housed in several decentralized operating companies around the world.

• We have strong competitive and economic incentives to move as quickly as possible toward a globally integrated model of operation: Each week we save in the development and registration process extends the commercial life of our patent protection and represents, at minimum, an additional $1 million in annual pretax profit—for each drug in our portfolio.

The previous case has five major elements that appear in most effective cases for action.

The *business context* summarizes and describes what is happening, what is changing, and what is newly important in the environment in which the company operates. Our leading competitors, this company's case for action says, are establishing much shorter development cycles.

The *business problem* is the source of the organizations concern. Our company, the document frankly admits, takes too long to develop and register new drugs.

The case for action also spells out *marketplace demands*—that is, how the contextual conditions have led to new performance requirements that the company can't meet. The competitive trend goes against our approach to research and development, this part says.

The *diagnostics* section of the case for action makes clear why the company is unable to meet the new performance requirements and why the usual fix-up, patch-up techniques of incremental improvement won't do. In this instance, the pharmaceutical company is losing its competitive edge to companies with globally integrated R&D organizations.

Finally, to eliminate any doubt about the need for reengineering, the case for action ends with a section that warns of the consequences of not reengineering, the *costs of inaction*. We stand to lose $1 million in annual profits, per drug, for every week's delay in development and registration, this part says.

A company doesn't have to teeter on the verge of bankruptcy to make a compelling case for reengineering. A case for action can be made even for a company that is doing well. Such an organization can argue that if it doesn't reengineer it *will* be in trouble, that it isn't as good as the market *will* demand that it be, or that it isn't as good as it has decided it *wants* to be. These are harder cases to make, which only means that the case for action has to be all the more compellingly argued.

Here's a case for action used by a consumer products company that is still profitable. The statement paints a dismal picture of the company's future if it doesn't reengineer. This case for action is longer than the pharmaceutical company's, but it is equally effective. It begins with an overview of the company's industry.

Case for Action
Consumer Products Company

• Markets are changing so quickly in our retail channels that, in order to generate profitable growth for our distributors, we must be able to respond quickly with exactly the right programs.

• Each of our channels has unique needs for innovative products, services, promotion, merchandising systems, and training to enable them to compete and succeed in their markets. We must develop the flexible processes within our company that thrive on these channel-specific opportunities.

• Consumer needs and desires are constantly changing, based on new retail formats, media stimulation, new products/substitute products, changing lifestyles, and market segmentation. We cannot develop a product concept or retail solution that appeals to everyone; products that are highly successful with one market segment will be rejected by another.

Next, it logically examines in competitive terms the factors that argue for change.

• Today, the time that elapses between our assessing a marketplace need and our delivery of a new program at retail is at least two years and can stretch out as long as three. Furthermore, the process is largely sequential. Each of the steps— interpreting retail and research data; developing plans; obtaining commitments; and getting agreement on product, merchandising, promotion, advertising, systems, training, and field-launch plans—crosses many division lines and requires endless meetings and approvals.

• In a dynamic market, a three-year planning cycle is unacceptable. Even if a product or program seems innovative in the early planning stages, it no longer is when it reaches the consumer twenty-four or thirty-six months later. Feedback on retail performance comes too late to affect replacement products and leaves poor performers in the market too long.

• Frequently, the scope of our planning and decision-making process is too narrow and does not encompass multiple channels or specific retailers. These are often left out or added late in the process, when our options are limited.

• Many times, when programs arrive at retail, the order is late, products and merchandising are missing and the retailer or field personnel lack enough training to effectively install or sell it.

The consumer product company's case winds up by emphatically stating the consequences of not reengineering:

• The current process is incapable of meeting our growing need for speed and precision. It produces, instead, a stressed and overworked staff, last-minute scrambles, increasing exception processing, and creaky systems. Our current process costs the company millions of dollars in overtime and excess expenses, missed deliveries, and less-than-acceptable retailer performance and confidence.

• We often place our focus on maximizing our own cost-effectiveness rather than on marketplace needs and performance. We have applied technology to improving what we do with little result. We have measured success by our own internal performance, rather than by our retailers' yardsticks.

• Just working harder and more efficiently within our existing process won't get us to our goal of dramatically improving retail performance.

• We're still very profitable today, but if we don't take comprehensive remedial actions soon, our continued success is at risk. Without major change, we will eventually fail.

This company's case for action, incidentally, led to a comprehensive and effective reengineering effort.

We have said there are two key components of the larger message that senior management has to communicate to the organization to get reengineering underway. The first is the "let's change" part—the case for action; the second is "to what"—the vision.

The case for action paints with a broad brush the nature of the company's business problem. "We have to get change going," it says. The vision says, "Here is what we want to be." It depicts the destination of the reengineering effort.

The vision statement, by that or any other name, is the way a company's management communicates a sense of the kind of organization the company needs to become. It describes how the company is going to operate and outlines the kind of results it must achieve. It is both a qualitative and a quantitative statement, which a company can use again and again before and during reengineering, as a reminder of reengineering's objectives, as a yardstick for measuring progress, and as a prod to keep the reengineering action going.

Creating the vision of a reengineered organization requires some artistry, because a vision is an image without great detail. When a company is taking its first steps toward reengineering, no one really knows exactly where it is heading; no one really knows exactly what it will become; no one really even knows which aspects of the current company will change, let alone precisely how. The vision is what a company believes it *wants* to achieve when it is done, and a well-drawn vision will sustain a company's resolve through the stress of the reengineering process.

The vision can act as a flag around which to rally the troops when morale starts to sag. "Remember how great it will be when we get there," the flag says to them. The vision also provides a continuing focus. It reminds people constantly of what it is the company is trying to change. Otherwise, people easily become sidetracked and diverted. In any company at any time, countless procedures and organizational details exist that *could* be changed. The vision reminds the organization which processes will actually need to be worked.

Finally, the vision provides a yardstick for measuring the progress of reengineering. Does the company look like its vision yet? If it is getting closer, reengineering is making progress. If not, then no matter how much effort has gone into reengineering, it hasn't created the progress on which the company is counting. Holding up the vision, the leader can say, "This is what we have agreed we want to be. Look around. Are we there yet? Are we close?" The vision is a useful prod. And, if it's really powerful, it creates a pull.

By working with companies that are reengineering their processes, we have expressed vision statements in some corny but effective ways. For instance, with desktop publishing it is easy to dummy up a *Wall Street Journal* article about the company written, say, five years hence. The story we write might say that the company has achieved record profits and jumped to the top of its industry by dramatically shortening its product development cycle. Then the story might spin out how it feels to work for the company and what customers and employees think about the changes it has made. This kind of device captures employees' imaginations. "Yes," they say, "we would like that." Well, that is the dream, the leader can say, and here is what we have to do to make it real.

Used together, the case for action and the vision work like a wedge and a magnet. To get people to move from where they are to where they are supposed to be requires two actions. First, they have to get unstuck from where they are. The tool that unsticks people is a wedge—the case for action. Next, the unstuck people have to be attracted to another point of view. That is the job of a magnet—the vision.

Vision statements need not be long, but they have to be powerful. Too many corporate visions tend to the vacuous and simplistic and provide no clue as to what the company must do to achieve them. "We want to be number one in our industry" or "we want to be the premier manufacturer of widgets" or "we will be the preferred supplier for our customers" are nice wishes, but they are not useful visions. Statements such as these often stem from the annual walk in the woods—those occasions when company executives go on retreat, claim to reexamine their purpose, and draw up what they term a vision statement. Although they are well intended, such statements are devoid of any real meaning. They don't suggest concretely how the company wants to operate, they have no real utility, and they wear off very quickly.

A powerful vision contains three elements that a product of a walk in the woods usually lacks. First, it focuses on operations; second, it includes measurable objectives and metrics; and third, if it is really powerful, it changes the basis for competition in the industry.

One of the best and simplest examples of a vision we know was expressed by Federal Express in its infancy: "We will deliver the package by 10:30 the next morning." That statement is about operations (we will get the package delivered); it has measurable objectives (we will deliver it by 10:30 A.M.); and it changed the basis of competition in the industry (from long, unpredictable delivery times to guaranteed overnight delivery). Federal Express' vision statement told people in the company that they had to design their work to accomplish that objective.

Vision statements can be much longer, as the samples below illustrate, without being soft. These sample vision statements have sharp edges, they contain no platitudes, and they include the three key elements we have just discussed. Here, to start, is the pharmaceutical company's vision of its drug development process in its reengineered incarnation.

VISION
PHARMACEUTICAL COMPANY

- We are a worldwide leader in drug development

  — We have shortened drug development and registration by an average of six months
  — We are an acknowledged leader in the quality of registration submissions
  — We have maximized the profit potential of our development portfolio

- We have created, across our operating companies, a worldwide R&D organization with management structures and systems that let us mobilize our collective development resources responsively and flexibly.

— We have established uniform and more disciplined drug development planning, decision-making, and operational processes across all sites
— We employ innovative technology-based tools to support our work and management practices at all levels and between all R&D sites
— We have developed and implemented a common information technology architecture worldwide

The consumer products firm whose case for action we looked at earlier has also articulated its end-state vision.

VISION
CONSUMER PRODUCTS FIRM

• Operating close to the marketplace injects a new life into the entire product development process. We develop plans, make decisions, produce products, and launch programs with a sense of immediacy. Our employees are rewarded by seeing products in stores that they worked on weeks or months but not years ago.

• Our market focus is sharpened because our fully integrated programs are never more than a year away from market. The needs of our marketplace drive us, and we evaluate our success by our performance at retail—retail sales, retail profitability, retail service, and retail execution.

• Cross-divisional teams working simultaneously streamline the development planning process. Priorities are consistent across all divisions as we focus our efforts on programs that move the needle. We set clear objectives, and market research provides immediate feedback on how well we performed against these objectives.

• The freshness of our product offering and the cohesive merchandising presentation and execution give all our retailers a competitive edge. Our field organization and accounts are fully trained in the process of implementation and in the strategies supporting our programs so that they can sell to their customers knowledgeably and enthusiastically.

• Our retailers can see that our programs are forward-looking, aggressive, and right for them. They notice the impact on their sales and profits immediately. Our products arrive complete, on time, and packed for efficient check-in and set up. Those responsible for merchandising these products have all the necessary tools and training. The partnership between us and our retailers is so strong that we work toward the same objectives and the same measures of success.

We have said that preparing and disseminating the case for action and the vision is the first step in reengineering. It is the leader's personal responsibility to articulate and communicate these key messages. It is only an individual with the leader's seniority and clout who can fashion and communicate these critical arguments.

The senior management team—the leader's peers or reports—represent the first audience for these messages. These messages are not easy for them to hear, since they say that the organization these people head is in need of major change. Only a very senior executive has the credibility and the clout to make such an assertion. An outside agent—a consultant—can be of help in this step, since an agent has no biases or vested interests and can be seen as an objective third party. Telling senior managers that their company is broken is difficult, since they have, in fact, played a substantial role in creating the current company, so diplomacy as well as credibility are important in communicating the case for action and the vision to them.

After senior management hears these messages, the rest of the organization must get the word, too. The case for action and the vision are the opening salvos in an ongoing communication barrage to enlist the entire organization in the reengineering crusade.

In the following four chapters, we will look at four very different companies and see how they have been able to launch and sustain successful reengineering efforts.

CHAPTER 10

ONE COMPANY'S EXPERIENCE— HALLMARK

No two companies' business situations are identical, and no two companies will tackle reengineering in just the same way. We are continually intrigued by the ingenuity and imagination that people in different companies apply to their reengineering efforts. The only absolutely essential element in every reengineering project is that it be directed at a process rather than a function. So long as that commandment is honored, practically everything else in reengineering comes down to technique— which is to say that it is *right* if it works for you and *wrong* if it does not.

Consequently, we thought the best way to close this book would be to let readers share in the experiences of some of reengineering's pioneers, people who have already been through a program or are currently in its throes of reinventing work in their companies. If the circumstances of these four cases, which are presented in the words of the people who actually did the reengineering, do not match those of your company, the cases nonetheless carry a message that should encourage and perhaps even inspire you. They show that real people in real businesses can apply the principles that we have articulated to produce extraordinary business results. The stories come from transcripts of conversations that we have had with the individuals who are narrating them. We have slightly edited some of their remarks for brevity or clarity.

We begin with the experiences of Robert L. Stark of Hallmark Cards, Inc., because in one respect it is the most striking. Of the four, Hallmark was the only company that was doing just fine when it decided to reengineer—not in response to any life-threatening problem but in a farsighted effort to keep such problems out of the company's future. For Hallmark, reengineering was a preemptive competitive strike.

Hallmark Cards, Inc. dominates the U.S. greeting card industry, and its products face little threat from non-U.S. competitors. Yet, the eighty-three-year-old Kansas City company is reengineering almost every aspect of its operations with the objective of dramatically reducing the time that elapses from noting a new market need to filling it with a card on the retailer's shelf. One of the biggest challenges facing Bob Stark, president of Hallmark's Personal Communications Group (PCG), was motivating the company to reengineer in the absence of a crisis. "It's a lot easier to rally your constituents when there is a clear and present danger," says Stark, who nonetheless managed to get Hallmark executives excited about the prospect of reengineering.

Stark is no wild-eyed radical. He joined Hallmark in 1958 and came up through the ranks. In 1984, he was named to head the company's core business, now called the PCG, which includes the Hallmark and Ambassador brands as well as Binney & Smith, a Hallmark subsidiary and maker of Crayola crayons. He became president in 1988. By that time, rapid change in the greeting-card market was already underway. Here's how he puts it:

> Our markets and channels of distribution had been reasonably ho-
> mogeneous for a long period of time. But in the 1980s, consumers
> started fragmenting into many, many groups and, simultaneously,
> our channels of distribution were expanding. Our eleven thousand-

plus specialty retailers faced higher downtown and mall rents, which meant they had to move more product, faster. Major retailers such as Wal-Mart and K Mart were also demanding tailored product and marketing programs from our Ambassador division for each of their thousands of stores.

By 1989, the huge proliferation of products in our line—a result of our focusing on smaller and smaller niches—had become apparent to us. The number of stock-keeping units was expanding far faster than our sales rate. Our average printing run sizes were falling, and that fact changed the economics of our business.

A large printing, die-cutting, or embossing press requires a lot of "make-ready" time—getting the press ready, the dies aligned, and so on. In the old days, eight hours to get a press ready and twenty to twenty-four hours to run the job was considered a reasonable ratio of make-ready to run time. When run time came down to eight hours and make-ready still came to eight hours, we had a very serious out-of-balance condition, with all kinds of implications for costs and capital.

Suddenly, you don't have capacity. You're running the same number of total units, but you need more presses. A large press can cost nearly $1 million, so if you suddenly need twenty to thirty more of them, your capital base extends significantly. Early on, we concluded that we couldn't live with those make-ready ratios.

What's more, we knew the problem would only get worse. To grow at our historical rates, we needed new and more lines of cards and related products to accommodate more market segments, as well as marketing and promotional programs tailored to our different channels. In addition, when market segments are less homogeneous, you have to respond to those segments faster, which means you have less time to figure out which products are winners and which are losers. But when your product offering broadens that much, your historical basis for forecasting sales is suddenly in jeopardy. So we needed new forecasting tools for new segments and faster feedback from the retail marketplace.

In February 1989, I convened an off-site meeting of forty senior executives to address these issues. This wasn't just a soul-searching session. We knew we had to talk about the *processes* by which we did business—what parts we thought we were good at and what we weren't. For those parts that we didn't think we were good at, we wanted to visualize what the future might look like in light of our concerns about stock number proliferation, movements in channels, and so on.

It was clear to us that major gaps existed between the way the company operated and where it had to go. Getting a new line of greeting cards from concept to market was taking two to three years. Costly revisions to designs, lettering and printing stock were numbering around fifty thousand per year. Once products were on the shelves, sales data often arrived too late—sometimes months later—to replenish the hot sellers, pull the slow ones, and plan for new lines. The window of opportunity can shut quickly in our business. Peak retail selling periods for major events such as Valentine's Day last only a few days, for example.

We also concluded that just doing a little bit better each year was not going to solve our problems. We had been improving a functionally oriented company for some time. But if we were going to make real breakthroughs and change the fundamental way we did business, the changes would have to occur across all these functions. It required a level of connection and cooperation that had not been required in the past.

It was my conviction, and that of the members of our operating committee, that the future was not going to look like the past and that the solutions of the past were not likely to work in the future. The continual refinements—tweaking each and every departmental task—would no longer be enough. Only a radical change in the way we did business could address our issues.

We needed to define clearly what we needed to accomplish and to assess our business priorities. We also needed to get everyone to understand what we were about in order to get everyone signed on. Initially, it's tough for people to get their mind around the concept of business reengineering. Once they do and they see something tangible, they get very enthused about it. Coming out of the chute, it seems you're never going to get a common understanding of what the issues are.

It was obvious early on that ours had to be a company-wide effort because it required cross-divisional teamwork of a magnitude we had never experienced before. Personally, it took me a little while to fully comprehend the significance of a truly company-wide, cross-divisional reengineering of our basic business processes. There's a great deal of difference between saying those words and understanding what they mean.

We were looking for major changes in the way Hallmark operated: how our artists, editors and other creative people worked together to conceive new products; how sales data was collected and used to improve product replenishment, marketing, and promotional campaigns; how we could manage graphics production and printing costs in the face of our proliferating products; and how we could satisfy the needs of ever-demanding, larger retailers. To underline the magnitude of the changes, we called the corporate transformation we were about to undergo "The Journey."

The operating committee and I spent a lot of time trying to understand the questions. After that, our challenge was communications: How do you get thousands of people to understand what you are talking about? We had to go through a definition of terms, come up with a lexicon, and go to great lengths to define the issues very clearly.

We found we had to codify and write down our beliefs, values, and strategic goals and how they related to our business priorities. What we were doing was, in fact, directly related to improving our performance in the marketplace. Linking all those elements together in a way that more than a handful of people could understand was a formidable challenge. It was a major, major hurdle.

Also, before any changes to work flows and organization charts could begin, we had to articulate and communicate what would *not* change: our core values and beliefs. Hallmark is known in Kansas City for our charitable works and for our stability. We are considered a pillar of strength in the city's business community. Our people were concerned that in reengineering we were going to change the bedrock of the business, and without these beliefs and values as a foundation, our employees could feel we were abandoning our legacy.

We all felt that the only person who could convey our beliefs and values adequately was Donald J. Hall, the company's chairman and son of the founder. Accordingly, Don wrote five beliefs and four guiding values that were communicated to all twenty-two thousand Hallmark employees over several months through private and group meetings; articles in the company's internal magazine; and videos featuring Hall, CEO Irvine Hockaday, Jr. and other senior executives. Once we had effectively communicated this message, everyone understood that while we would change our ability to get to the market, we wouldn't change our beliefs and values. That for us was a critical first step to create a change process focused on results.

It was also difficult at first to understand the relationship between continuous improvement and business reengineering. We had people using those terms and confusing them. We recognized this problem early, because we would get a lot of perplexed looks from people in the audience.

Going through business reengineering requires a different skill set from the one most of us had been using before. We all had to sign on and get commitment from the senior executives of the group to devote time to reengineering. We soon found out it's not something one does in fifteen or twenty minutes a day. It's not something one does by dipping in and dipping out or going to a briefing twice a month.

I take some satisfaction and pride out of the fact that the operating committee recognized the level of talent and commitment reengineering would take. We agreed it was significant enough to devote whatever time and energy—both our own and our corporate staff's—were necessary to accomplish our goals. We had to formulate, agree upon, and internalize our common business priorities.

But saying that is one thing. Where the rubber meets the road is when you have to staff one of these operations. To the credit of the officers involved, they anted up some of our best and brightest. That sent a very clear signal to the organization that we were serious.

By April 1990, the company had formulated its business priorities. In time, we came up with a clear set of objectives. We wanted to get new products to the market in less than a year; produce products and promotional programs that consistently won over both buyers and retailers; and reduce costs with continued improvements in quality. It all boiled down to dramatically improving performance at the retail level for the long-standing Hallmark specialty stores, the major department stores and supermarket chains, pharmacies, and other outlets for Hallmark and Ambassador products.

The articulation of the business priorities had a great impact. The most powerful part of "The Journey" is explicitly showing how processes must change and that the change is driven by the common goal of improving performance at retail. That allows everyone to get on board.

That's not to say there weren't hurdles to overcome in getting our organizations to change: It's human nature to endorse change for everybody else. But talking about change in the abstract and significantly changing the way you or I perform our work are two different things. We needed to demonstrate the viability of some of our concepts and come out with significant wins. That required picking our pilot projects carefully. They had to be believable and reproducible in another area of the organization. The improvement had to be order-of-magnitude—something you couldn't get from continuous improvement, for example.

That's one of the things you have to overcome from the beginning—the belief that this is just a productivity improvement program, the notion that "all you really want is to make me work harder." You have to get the point across that you're looking for everyone to work smarter, not harder. Once we explained our business priorities, our people accepted our ideas on why and how the business needed to change.

Following that step, we grouped one hundred people into nine teams to address a series of "leverage points"—the critical parts of the business that we needed to change. Several months later, the teams presented some one hundred recommendations for redesigning business processes to Hallmark's five-person operating committee. The committee approved an initial group of a dozen concepts, which would be validated in the first phase of pilot projects.

Initially, we all believed that information technology would prove a vital ingredient to our effort, but we were taking that on faith. We didn't understand the ramifications of the technology for our business processes. I think Americans as a whole have a great deal of faith that more information is better than less, and we were in that camp. But, in the beginning, we couldn't get very specific about what information technology meant to the business and which areas offered the most leverage.

The specifics came with a recommendation to improve the flow of sales data from the Hallmark specialty stores to corporate headquarters. We outfitted 250 of the independently owned Hallmark stores with computerized point-of-sale systems that use barcodes to capture detailed information on every purchase. Since October 1991, we have been getting nearly instantaneous information on what's selling.

Making the torrent of data meaningful to our management was the next step. Five other groups made up of research and information systems people were set up to produce "decision-support" systems—computer programs that key executives could use to graphically interpret trends in the stores.

We all feel this retail information will be the new lifeblood of Hallmark. Knowing exactly what sold yesterday, where it sold, what it sold with, what part of the day it sold, and what display it came out of will make dramatic and exciting changes in our business.

Although we're still in the early stages of using the retail data, we believe it has already made a significant impact by dramatically supporting some of our intuition about the operations of the stores. For instance, we found that during the Christmas season, our stores should offer an even broader line of holiday goods. We also quantified which products sell better when they are adjacent to other products.

In the past, we would have been leery about suggesting major product and format changes to the retailers. We might have waited perhaps twenty-four months before we said anything. But now when we tell our retailers what works and what doesn't, we're doing it with retail—not wholesale—data.

The ability to track the effectiveness of a store layout or advertising campaign more precisely and quickly will reshape the way we merchandise and market. If we can sell a product line just as well without some fancy display, we can put that money toward something that has leverage.

Another point we had to communicate during "The Journey" was the fact that time truly is money and that probably the single best way to save money is to save time. That was a real breakthrough for us; we didn't realize how much inefficiency was in the system simply due to queue time. That was never a problem in the past. You always had time to do things over if you didn't do it right the first time.

For example, in our lengthy product development cycle, the majority of the time wasn't spent in printing and production. Rather, two-thirds of the cycle was spent in developing the plan and the concept and in the creative part.

Our company has the largest creative staff in the world—seven hundred artists and writers who create more than twenty-three thousand product designs each year. The process that begins with assessing a marketplace need and ends with a new product line has been largely sequential. It's required numerous meetings, many changes to editorial and artwork, and countless approvals and back-and-forth as we pursued the memorable product. One study found that from the time a concept was given to the creative staff to the time it hit the printing department, there were twenty-five handoffs. And 90 percent of that time involved work sitting in someone's in- or out-basket.

In the summer of 1991, we developed a new line of cards in an entirely different way. We grouped people together who had been separated by disciplines, departments, floors, and even buildings to cut down on the queue time, spur creativity and end the throw-it-over-the-wall-it's-their-problem cycle.

These experiments in integrated teams worked so well that half of the line hit the stores by September—eight months ahead of schedule. The other half were test marketed in the spring. We were so encouraged by the initial successes in new-card development that we decided to put development efforts for our seasonal products—about 40 percent of our business—on schedules of less than a year.

We think the teams worked because by bringing a group of people together like that, they get focused and you get direct communications linkages. In addition, probably the most rewarding experiences for the artists and writers is seeing their work in its final form much earlier. It gives them instant gratification.

We made changes to the review process as well. In the old routine, a management committee periodically reviewed the artists' and editors' work. In the integrated teams, the team reviews its own work. If they start out knowing management's philosophy and understand that management will look at it in the end, the team doesn't need all the interim reviews. As a result, the process goes much faster, and we are turning out a better product.

We still have plenty of challenges as "The Journey" continues. A major one is acceptance. As business processes are accelerated, our people need to understand that we aren't asking them to take quality out of the product. If it really adds value to the consumer, then we want to put more of it in. But that isn't always the same as adding cost.

Another challenge is technological. As a result of the business process changes, Hallmark will need more advanced information systems, like the point-of-sale technology we installed at the Hall-mark stores. Point-of-sale information also flows in from mass-channel accounts served by Ambassador. Because all of the business process redesign pilot programs have technology people on the team, the technology piece is being designed in.

What makes this process exciting is that it is a once-in-a-lifetime opportunity. We are building the organizational capability that will enable Hallmark employees to react swiftly and successfully to con-tinuous, unpredictable change.

We could never go back to the old way of doing business. More important, I believe everyone involved knows that this is a never ending process, that we truly have adopted a new way of doing business.

At the beginning, when I would talk to employee groups about all the changes we had put in place, I would get questions like "When are things going back to normal?" My answer was, "This is nor-mal." The pace and the change are the new norm. I don't get those questions any more.

One thing I want to stress: We concluded early in the game that this was a top-down process, not something that was likely to reach critical mass on its own or something that would bubble up. Contin-uous improvement can do that—bubble up from a unit and reach critical mass of its own volition. We knew that because of the cross-divisional and cross-functional nature of this effort, it had to be driven top-down.

When you drive something from the top, you have to articulate clearly and communicate why it is being done. That's why we started with our beliefs and values as an organization, then moved to our vision, and linked it to our business priorities to get everyone work-ing toward the same objectives.

It is crucial to have people understand that their functional unit could have objectives that seem valid yet might not be aligned with overall business priorities. That took some persuasion.

If you can agree on your business priorities and focus the energies of your people on them, it's amazing what happens. When everyone in the organization feels responsible for the success of the total enterprise and knows how they can contribute, you have achieved empowerment.

I was in Japan a couple of months ago for the first time in many years. It's perfectly clear while you're there why the Japanese are such a competitive force: That whole country is focused. They know they are in an economic battle that they intend to win. They have a homogeneous society all marching to the same drummer. Everybody you talk to over there knows what their company and their country are about. They are aligned, and it's a powerful force.

In that respect we at Hallmark were lucky because of our culture. At the start we determined that what we were really talking about is empowering our people to be the very best they could be, to provide an effective working environment for every employee in the organization, regardless of his or her role. We want them to feel the satisfaction that comes with knowing that they made a difference. We want to provide them with the vehicle and the focus that allows that to happen.

One of the things I enjoy the most—and I don't get a chance to do it often enough—is to tour our manufacturing facilities. I really like talking to the people who are implementing things. All you have to do is talk to our people on the plant floors about the things they are doing, the teams they are affiliated with, and the work cells they are involved with. They tell you it is much more fulfilling to come to work. You come back feeling really good about what you see and hear.

As the new business processes are implemented, the biggest challenge ahead is not allocation of resources. We've already made the call that we will allocate whatever resources are required. I suspect that the challenge on the roll-outs will be staying the course, because we know that roll-outs under the new process will not be uneventful.

I am sure there will be concerns expressed about unanticipated problems. We believe we have assessed as best we know how the magnitude of the risks and have balanced the risk to reward ratios. In situations where it appears we have underestimated the challenge, there will be a tendency not to stay the course. That's where leadership comes in.

We all appreciate the significance of the changes ahead, but we're confident it will be a rewarding journey. No one is sitting around biting their nails and fretting that we are about to march off the edge of a cliff. On the other hand, we aren't a bunch of starry-eyed dreamers who believe we can do anything. We're pretty realistic and confident about what we can do. Whatever the challenges, we are confident that we will meet them.

Bob Stark's narrative of Hallmark's reengineering experience points up three things that senior managers too often overlook or underemphasize. First is the cardinal and continuing need to communicate, communicate, communicate so that everyone in the organization understands the method and goals of the reengineering effort. Business reengineering and process thinking are not easy concepts to grasp. People at every level of the company have to "get it" before reengineering can work, but this is especially true for the management team, which can easily block reengineering when it begins to intrude on their turf and prerogatives. Talking at people serves no purpose if they're not hearing or not *understanding* what they're hearing, which is why the leader of a reengineering effort must check often to make sure the message he or she is sending is in fact the one that's getting through.

Second, the Hallmark case shows how important it is not just to get senior management's concurrence, but to get them to commit themselves and their *best* people to the effort.

Third, Hallmark established clear goals. Stark and others responsible for the effort didn't say we want to be the best we can. Instead, they said, in less than a year we want to accomplish this, this, and this. At the same time, they clearly understand that reengineering is not a completely planned activity. Hallmark didn't know at the beginning precisely how it was going to proceed. They expected there would be unanticipated problems, and there have been.

Finally, the case illustrates Hallmark management's understanding and appreciation that reengineering is not a one-time trip. It is a never ending journey, because the world keeps changing. Processes that have been reengineered once will someday have to be reengineered all over again. Reengineering is not a project; it must be a way of life.

CHAPTER 11

ONE COMPANY'S EXPERIENCE— TACO BELL

The Taco Bell subsidiary of PepsiCo was sick and getting sicker when John E. Martin was named CEO in 1983. Martin's problem was not convincing people that the company had to reengineer for the long-term future. His problem was getting change that was radical enough and soon enough to save the company. Martin had inherited the leadership of a company that was becoming smaller and less profitable by the day. Here's what John Martin recently had to say about the changes he initiated at Taco Bell.

For us, the process of reengineering has been like a voyage of discovery—a voyage we have been on now for nearly a decade, and one that we realize will continue as long as Taco Bell is in the business of serving customers.

Throughout the entire process, our greatest insight has been our most basic—namely, that everything begins with a simple decision to listen to our customer.

When I became CEO in 1983, Taco Bell was much like every other quick-service restaurant business. We were a top-down, "command-and-control" organization with multiple layers of management, each concerned primarily with bird-dogging the layers below them. We were also process-driven, in the old sense of the word, with operational handbooks for everything—including, literally, handbooks to interpret other handbooks.

Like our competitors, we were caught up in the process of processing; we were striving for bigger, better, and more complicated in just about everything we did.

If something was simple, we made it complex. If it was hard, we figured out a way to make it impossible.

We operated this way, because with all our layers of management, we needed to make things difficult so we could keep everybody busy. The more commands and controls we had in the system, the more the system justified its own existence.

Unfortunately, in our ever-increasing efforts to micromanage every aspect of restaurant operations, we became so focused on ourselves and our processes that we forgot to ask a basic question: What the heck do our customers think about all this?

Did they care that our assistant restaurant managers could assemble and disassemble the twelve parts of a deep fryer with a blindfold on? Did they care that somebody in our industry probably wrote a handbook on it, including recommendations for the type of blindfold to use? Did they care, in the final analysis, that we managed to turn the relatively simple business of fast food into rocket science, all under the presumption that it was good for them?

Even before taking over as chief executive officer, I had a notion that our customers didn't give a hoot about any of our elaborate systems. My appointment as CEO gave me an opportunity to prove it. It's important to remember that back in the early 1980s, Taco Bell was very much a regional Mexican-American restaurant chain that had enjoyed a fair degree of success in a relatively small niche. In 1982, we had fewer than 1,500 restaurants and did $500 million in total sales; our major competitors, mostly in the hamburger business, were light years ahead of us.

The fast-food world was passing Taco Bell by. In fact, our cumulative real growth from 1978, when PepsiCo acquired Taco Bell, to 1982 was a negative 16 percent compared to the total industry's positive 6 percent.

We were going backwards—fast.

The problem was Taco Bell really didn't know what it wanted to be in those days. So our first order of business was to create a vision for the company. Since we had no place to go but up, we decided to think the unthinkable and create a vision of Taco Bell as a giant in the fast-food industry—not just the leader in the Mexican category, but a competitive force with which all restaurant organizations in all categories would have to contend.

A lot of restaurant people, including many in our own organization, thought that our new vision was something more than far-sighted. Farfetched was a word we heard often. But Taco Bell was in an "up or out" situation; there was only one thing we knew for sure, and that was we had to change in a very big way.

Nowadays, when I think back to that early vision and to the massive amount of change we've had to create to fulfill it, I'm reminded of something Robert Kennedy once said: "Progress is a nice word. But change is its motivator, and change has its enemies." His point was that you can't get from Point A to Point B without dealing with some problems.

For Taco Bell to progress from a regional Mexican-American restaurant chain to a national force in the industry, we had to accept the fact that our greatest enemies were the tradition-bound ideas to which many of our employees clung.

In those days, traditional thinkers believed they knew what customers wanted without even asking *them*. Fancier decors, bigger kitchens, more sophisticated equipment, larger staffs, broader menus, outdoor playgrounds. Without asking our customers, in other words, we assumed that what they wanted was bigger, better, and more complex. By following through on this tradition-bound thinking, we were providing slower and costlier service.

So we began our voyage by asking our customers what *they* wanted, and what we found out was encouraging. Our customers, it turned out, didn't want any of those bigger, better, fancier things we assumed they did. What they really wanted was very simple: good food, served fast and hot, in a clean environment, at a price they could afford.

That was it. All the rest meant little to them.

The initial research we did at Taco Bell became our declaration of independence. It helped us look at Taco Bell in an entirely different way and allowed us to turn customer value into the key element of our business proposition.

When a customer walks into a quick-service restaurant and gives us a dollar, a large part of what he or she is paying for has nothing to do with what the customer actually receives for the money. Sure, all the cost factors are important from a business point of view. But what's important from the customer's point of view? Is labor important? No. Is rent important? Not unless you're a PepsiCo shareholder.

In the end, the only important category to customers is food and paper, because that's what they get back for the dollar they give us. Amazingly, though, the percentage of his or her dollar the customer pays for food and paper—in other words, the cost of goods sold—is, historically, the one variable chains have tried to reduce. Even today, restaurant people brag about holding food and paper costs down to twenty-five or twenty-six cents, and putting the extra pennies into marketing, which accounts for about eight cents out of every customer dollar.

One of our well-known, fast-food competitors spends about $1 billion a year marketing its business. That's the cost of about eight billion bean burritos, enough to give every person on this planet one and a half burritos free every year.

So we decided to reduce everything but our cost of goods sold, including the cost of marketing. If we created a better deal for the consumer, we thought, perhaps we wouldn't have to pay so much to twist people's arms to get them to buy our product.

With that decision, we were creating a true paradigm shift that launched our entire reengineering process.

I cannot tell you how exciting and liberating that shift was for our company. By thinking entirely outside the box, by saying to ourselves that the old methods were the way of the dinosaur, we unleashed a power within our company that has produced enormous success, and, in fact, has enabled us now to think realistically about becoming the dominant force in the convenient food industry within the next ten years. Our initial vision has a good chance of becoming reality. Not bad for a sleepy little Mexican-American restaurant organization.

How was that power manifested in the reengineering process?

It took several forms—including a complete reorganization of our

human resources and a dramatic redesign of our operational systems
to make them more innovative and customer focused.

By traditional restaurant standards the reengineering of our management processes was radical. We eliminated entire layers of management and, in the process, completely redefined nearly every job in
the system.

For example, we did away with the "district manager" supervisory layer, which traditionally oversees the management of five or
six restaurants. By eliminating that job category, we dramatically
changed the job description of our restaurant managers, who had
previously reported to the district managers.

For the first time in the fast-food industry, we told restaurant
managers that they were responsible for running their own operations without the help—or the hindrance—of another layer of supervision. "You're in charge now," we told them. "How your unit
performs in terms of sales, profitability, and customer satisfaction is
in your hands, and we will evaluate your performance and decide
your compensation based on those very specific business indica-
tors." That was an unheard of move for the command-and-control,
quick-service restaurant industry.

The reorganization proved painful for some managers, especially
those who still believed the ultimate test of their abilities was assembling the deep-fryer blindfolded. Many managers, however, adapted
easily and immediately to the new approach. In fact, they responded
so well that eventually we changed their job title from restaurant
manager to restaurant general manager. Since they were each responsible for a $1 million to $2 million a year business, they were
clearly operating in a general management capacity.

For several years after this reorganization, we saw an exodus of
the traditional thinking managers. Most, in fact, wound up working
in management positions with our competition, where the area
supervisor who oversees a span of five restaurants is still very much
the norm.

By contrast, at the Taco Bell supervisory level, our reorganization
produced an entirely new job category that we call "market manager." This position exists nowhere else in the restaurant industry.

In 1988, Taco Bell had about 350 area supervisors controlling
about 1,800 restaurants. Today, we have just over 100 market
managers responsible for about 2,300 company-owned restaurants.

Market managers each oversee at least 20 restaurants. Some are in charge of 40, which if you know the restaurant business, you know is an enormous responsibility.

Successful market managers in the new Taco Bell manage by exception, which means they must work only to solve problems, not create them. Equally important, they have to completely reject the old command-and-control style in favor of a model that promotes flexibility, relies on the most advanced management information systems in the business, encourages innovation, and empowers the people around them to do their jobs.

The new market manager position prompted a shake out, as had the previous change.

Some former area supervisors rose to the new challenge, others switched to restaurant general managers and became very productive, while still others left Taco Bell for the more comfortable confines of our competitors.

Several of those who left, in fact, took me aside and said, in effect, "Hey, John, you're out in left field without a mitt. This new Taco Bell will never work. There are too many changes."

Each time I would listen, smile, shake their hand, and thank them for being an important part of Taco Bell's successful *past*.

After each of those conversations, I was more committed to the reengineering process than ever. Why? Because at Taco Bell, we had accepted that even though change could be painful, it was also an inevitable byproduct of growth and success. It is when people *stop* taking me aside and saying, "John, these changes will never work," that I'm going to start worrying, because that's when Taco Bell is starting to stagnate.

The great American author John Steinbeck once wrote, "It is the nature of man as he grows older to protest against change, particularly change for the better." To understand the truth of that statement, just take a hard look at America's electronics industry, our once great railroad industry, and the struggling steel and auto manufacturers. They all grew comfortable in their old age, resisted the inevitability of change, and are now paying the consequences. Which is precisely why I say the reengineering process at Taco Bell is a never ending process of change and renewal.

Change begets change, and so at the same time we were reorganizing our management resources, we had to rethink everything else we did. Throughout the total reengineering effort, we maintained just one simple rule—enhance those things that bring value to the customers and change or eliminate those that don't.

We have to accept the fact that we are not in the same business we were in during the sixties and seventies. The old ways don't apply, and we must change every aspect of our business accordingly.

Take, for example, our Taco Bell restaurant buildings. To enhance value to our customer, and to eliminate what we didn't need, we had to completely reengineer them. Before 1983, a typical Taco Bell restaurant was comprised of 70 percent kitchen and 30 percent customer area. Like everybody else in the industry, we had complicated our operations to the point where our internal needs were pushing the customer out the door. Today, after eight years of reengineering, we have turned the situation around. Our new restaurants average 30 percent kitchen and 70 percent customer area. We've been able to double the number of seats within the same square footage as our older style building.

Our competitors' units, by the way, have become bigger and bigger, while ours have stayed the same size. A new full-sized Taco Bell restaurant, including seating, could fit into the *kitchen* space of some of our typical fast-food hamburger competitors.

Moreover, our downsizing of the kitchen area hasn't hurt productivity one bit. In fact, it's done just the opposite. In the early 1980s, when our kitchens used to make up 70 percent of the total restaurant space, we considered peak capacity for a top unit to be about $400 per hour. Today, our top restaurants have a peak capacity of $1,500 per hour. Moreover, our average pricing today is about 25 percent lower than it was nine years ago.

What we have achieved through reengineering is a synergy of all our processes. As our value-based marketing strategy drives sales and transactions, our efforts at reengineering make those sales more profitable, and, at the same time, increase the customer satisfaction ratings we track on a continual basis.

Other reengineering success stories for us have been a system we call K-Minus, a program we call TACO, or Total Automation of Company Operations, and some of our latest out of the box thinking in alternative points of distribution and applied technology. Let me explain.

K-Minus, which stands for a kitchenless restaurant, evolved from our belief that we are a customer-driven, retail service company, *not* a manufacturing company. We believe our restaurants should *retail* food, not *manufacture* it.

Today, our meat and beans are cooked outside the restaurant at central commissaries; all we need is hot water to reheat the ingredients for serving. We also K-Minus the preparation of our corn shells and cheese, as well as all the dicing and chopping of lettuce, tomatoes, onions, and olives.

So far, the results from K-Minus have been outstanding. We've already pushed fifteen hours of work per day out of the restaurant, which translates system-wide to about eleven million hours per year.

Taco Bell saved about $7 million from K-Minus just last year. We also benefited from greater quality control, better employee morale (because we eliminated most of the drudgery of food preparation), fewer employee accidents and injuries, big savings in utilities, and, of course, more time to focus on the customer.

The TACO system gives each restaurant a level of MIS sophistication that is unparalleled in the fast-food industry. That system puts the power of computer technology in the hands of our people, promoting self-sufficiency, and eliminating thousands of hours of paperwork and administrative time that are better spent directly serving our customers.

Equally important, programs like K-Minus and TACO serve as agents of change for even more advanced ideas, such as alternative points of distribution and new technology. Here's what I mean:

When people look at a classic, free-standing Taco Bell restaurant, they see something that in the future could just as easily be a McDonald's, a Burger King, or any other competitor. It is a building, comprised of bricks and mortar, glass and assorted restaurant equipment, and for the past thirty or forty years it has both defined and confined who and what we are.

Defined and confined because inside those four walls, our target audience is people who eat at fast-food restaurants. Outside those walls, our target audience is people who eat. Inside the walls, the total market is $78 billion. Outside the walls, the total market is the sum of all meal occasions, or about $600 billion, in the United States alone.

When we started to redefine ourselves in terms of what I like to call the total share of stomach, we began to look at our bricks-and-mortar restaurant as just one point of distribution in a universe of many distribution points.

Moreover, we stopped confining ourselves to the goal of becoming the value leader in the quick-service restaurant industry and set our sights on a new goal: to become the value leader for all foods for all meal occasions.

So we're knocking down those traditional walls, and taking our food to places where people congregate. Right now, these include corporate and industrial dining centers, schools and universities, airports, and stadiums. I'm happy to report that those new distribution points are all doing great, but as far as I'm concerned they're just a start.

The real promise comes from the points of distribution we haven't discovered yet. That's because reengineering brings about change, change produces new ideas, and new ideas result in growth. For Taco Bell, the growth has been sensational. Since 1989, sales have increased by 22 percent per year. This exceptional sales growth has been driven by increased transactions, the best indicator of our success.

In terms of profit growth, Taco Bell has averaged earnings increases of 31 percent since 1989, which is incredible when you take into account the enormous financial investments we've made in technology, organizational changes, and power building our company. Our huge profit growth is happening at a time when the rest of this industry is struggling to increase profits at all.

And because of our continuing efforts to reengineer our operations and to think of our growth not in terms of four-walled restaurants but in terms of points of distribution, we expect these numbers to skyrocket in the years ahead. Vending machines, supermarkets, schools, retail outlets, street corners—you name it, we'll be there. In fact, we're confident that in the next decade, Taco Bell will have tens of thousands of points of distribution, which is a long, long way from the current 3,600 restaurants we now operate. We'll get there, because if we don't, somebody else will. That's the reality that drives our business, and constantly pushes us to think of unique opportunities to enhance customer value.

Another of those opportunities involves the application of new technology. Our guiding principle here, as everywhere else, is that every technical innovation we implement must simultaneously enhance service and reduce costs.

The progress we've made in implementing effective technology has been so outstanding that CBS News did a segment on our advances. Consider, for example, our taco-making machine. It can churn out up to nine hundred tacos an hour, all perfectly proportioned, all served at exactly the right temperature, all individually wrapped and ready to deliver to our customers. It has another plus, too; it shows up for work every day! In a real sense, our new taco-making machine serves as a symbol of the progress we've made through reengineering.

I remember vividly the day the idea was placed on the table just a couple of years ago. Sure, there was some snickering, and sure, there were people who thought the idea would never get off the ground. But that's okay, because the really important thing is that the *new* Taco Bell didn't let the *old* Taco Bell stand in the way of progress.

If we had let traditional thinking guide our actions, that taco-making machine would never exist today.

To sum up, Taco Bell went from being a $500 million regional company in 1982 to a $3 billion national company today all because we listen to our customers and are not afraid to change. I predict that by the year 2000, Taco Bell will be a $20 billion company, again, because we're a company that listens to our customers and is not afraid to change. When someone says to me—and they do—"John, that forecast is completely farfetched," I just keep in mind two things: First, when the traditional thinkers tell you your goal is farfetched, you're probably on to something big. Second, when they stop telling you it's farfetched, you've probably already lost the war.

John Martin's story is inspiring. His reengineering effort paid off magnificently as Taco Bell's sales soared from $500 million to $3 billion in an industry that is declining. Several points are worth underscoring in this case.

The most dramatically drawn lesson is Martin's recognition that the customer must be the starting point for everything in reengineering. In reconceptualizing the company's processes, Martin and his people always began with the customer's needs and worked backwards from there. This perspective stands in sharp contrast to that of the traditional manager who put fryer maintenance skills at the top of the list. Equipment maintenance is important, but it's not what customers are hoping for when they walk through Taco Bell's door. In the standard, bureaucratic company structure, people correlate their personal importance with the number of their direct reports or the value of the assets they control. This is one of the values that reengineering has to change, because it leads to the building of infrastructure—larger and more complicated kitchens—that doesn't serve customers' real needs. Taco Bell's reengineering was unambiguously customer-driven in that every change was tested against a standard: Does this add value for the customer?

Another lesson to come out of John Martin's experience: Expect resistance and be prepared to deal with it. People with a vested interest in the way things are will be upset when you change them. If some people are upset it's a good sign that you're doing something significant.

The Taco Bell case also illustrates the ripple effect we've discussed. Change a process, and that change ripples into other aspects of the organization. Taco Bell changed the food-assembly process, which precipitated a change in the managerial structure, which meant the company had to change its compensation system. Process change ripples into universal organizational change.

Finally, Taco Bell has made its corporate vision clear with that brilliant phrase, "We want to be number one in share of stomach." That statement tells anyone hearing or reading it that the company's opportunities are far greater than just selling Mexican fast food in sit-down restaurants. Every company that is reengineering should seek a phrase that is as clear, eloquent, and eye-opening as that one.

ONE COMPANY'S EXPERIENCE— CAPITAL HOLDING

Suppose that after you have spent years developing the perfect wristwatch—absolutely accurate and very inexpensive—the world began working on a twenty-three-hour day. Your watch was still an engineering marvel and kept great time, but it was a twenty-four-hour timepiece in a twenty-three-hour world. That is roughly analogous to what happened to Capital Holding Corporation's Direct Response Group (DRG), a direct marketer of insurance—life, health, property, and casualty—via television, telephone, and direct mail.

DRG had used celebrity spokespeople such as Lorne Greene, Michael Landon, Art Linkletter, and Roger Staubach to promote its products over late-night and daytime television. DRG fed millions of names into its high-volume, direct-mail machine and was an efficient factory for marketing on the averages, a one size fits all approach to selling insurance.

But while DRG was busy growing, the world began to change.

By the mid-1980s, the mass marketing machinery that had worked well for years was delivering DRG's creative pitches to overflowing consumer mailboxes, from which those pitches were increasingly likely to travel straight to the rubbish bin.

Direct-mail clutter was not DRG's biggest problem. Its marketing on the averages strategy was about to run headlong into the decade of the customer. That big, friendly bear that DRG used to call the mass market was turning into a monster with many heads, each with its own state of mind. Moreover, the mass media that used to reach the average consumer so efficiently had splintered into shards. Mainstream America did not exist any more, and people had more to watch than the big three television networks.

So there sat DRG—a world-class mass marketer with a disappearing mass market. New sales no longer offset the company's lapsed policies, so growth slowed. Response rates slipped, driving the cost per sale up, and margins began to erode to the detriment of the bottom line.

DRG's senior vice president, Pamela Godwin, picks up the story at this point.

In 1988, DRG president Norm Phelps and other senior executives decided that for our company, the days of mass marketing were over. They realized that to improve the company's value to the customer, to increase response rates, and to keep more customers on the book, we would have to strengthen DRG's relationships with existing customers and target our marketing to those potential customers whose profiles matched specific company strategies.

In other words, to remain in the direct response insurance business, DRG would have to offer customers service, not just products, and it would have to offer products designed to serve particular, identifiable classes of customers.

To that end, Phelps created a new vision for DRG. He decided that the company needed to be exactly what most people didn't expect it to be—an insurance company that cares about its customers and wants to give them the best possible value for their premium dollar.

The new vision statement is direct, unambiguous, and so compact that it fits easily on a single page.

CARING, LISTENING, SATISFYING . . . ONE BY ONE

Each of us is devoted to satisfying the financial concerns of every member of our customer family by:

• deeply caring about and understanding each member's unique financial concerns.

• providing value through products and services that meet each member's financial concerns.

• responding with the clear information, personal attention, and respect to which each member is entitled.

• nurturing an enduring relationship that earns each member's loyalty and recommendation.

To carry out our vision we must:

• find and serve people who have a strong sense of affiliation, reaching them through new or existing membership groups.

• provide our members with a broad range of insurance and savings products.

• communicate personally with each member through direct response, emphasizing telephone and technology to build close relationships.

Our unmatchable spirit of dedication to member satisfaction sets us apart. It is the promise on which current members rely, to which new members are attracted, and by which each of us lives.

The overall responsibility for translating this ambitious vision into reality was a massive undertaking. In 1988, I was asked to head a cross-functional team of middle and senior managers that would take the company's existing sales, service, and marketing processes apart and put them back together again in a new configuration. We wanted a customer-driven business model that would do two things. First, it had to allow us to sell and service existing customers better than any competitor. Second, it had to allow us to capture as much information as possible about our existing customers and apply that information to our marketing efforts.

The new configuration that this team created took the shape of a figure eight. The bottom loop we called customer management. The top loop, market management.

The bottom loop would deliver the new level of responsive, personalized service we were after. Customers would no longer get bounced from department to department and to people who are equipped to handle only one piece of their problem. Instead, this loop of the business model would depend on frontline teams that could handle any customer issue through the use of comprehensive, interactive, and user-friendly information systems. These same teams would be able to make sales to the company's existing customers while collecting useful information from those customers at every opportunity.

The upper loop of the figure eight—what we called market management—would use one of the largest proprietary databases in the country with detailed records on fifteen million consumers, active customers, former customers, and people who have inquired about the company's products. The information in that database comes from several sources. One is the lower half of the figure eight, the interaction with DRG's customers. Another source is commercial data providers. Also, DRG would link its database to powerful syndicated researchers who could help us cut the database into slivers and let us see quickly which products will interest which narrow groups. The upper loop uses the knowledge it acquires in order to create and market the company's products, and it supplies the lower loop with prospects and new customers.

That was the strategic business model that we wanted to create, and now, four years later, we are well along in reengineering the company. We knew then, however, that moving the company from what it was to what we wanted it to be wasn't a matter of just bending and shaping our old systems. We had to build new processes from the ground up. We had to change our business, not on our terms, but on the customer's terms. And we had to make those changes fast, while maintaining profitability and generating a return to Capital Holding shareholders. We had to create a step-by-step strategy for change. We had to reengineer, not just one process but everything the company did.

My role was the leader's role. My job was to help senior management create the new business model for DRG, and then to empower the teams—eventually there would be a dozen of them—that would reengineer specific processes inherent within the new model.

We knew from the vision statement what we wanted the company to be, but how, for instance, could we "respond with the clear information, personal attention, and respect to which each member is entitled," as the vision demanded, when we suffered from the curse of departmentalization. For instance, one of the processes DRG had to change was the way it handled insurance applications. Clerks passed the application from one stage to another until somebody got back to the customer. The only time anybody had any real responsibility for an application was when it happened to land on his or her desk. If we were going to match our performance to our vision, that had to change. So, among a great many other things, we're developing a new process in which individual case workers own the customer from the time an application comes in until the issue decision is made.

We had been told—and now we know it's true—that before you can effect any significant change, you've first got to understand your company's culture. People behave logically in the context of their environment, so if you want employees to change their behavior you've got to create an environment that's aligned with your business strategy. Therefore, the first thing we did before reengineering the insurance application process or any of the others was to conduct a cultural audit, which helped us discover and understand our employees' attitudes.

This was an important step for us but one that many companies might skip. We know now that it would have been impossible to reengineer our systems and processes without understanding the cultural barriers and the people issues that stood in our way.

Our cultural audit was a three-part affair. In the first, we hired an outside firm to conduct a standard employee attitude survey and report the results back to us. We tore their report apart and closely analyzed their findings.

For the second part, we put together what you could call a multi-level, cross-functional, cultural transformation team. It comprised twenty-five employees ranging from secretaries to vice presidents from every part of our existing organization. Their job was to get the real dirt on us as a company by means of interviews with frontline employees. We wanted to find out the unwritten rules in the organization. They asked questions such as, "If your younger brother or sister came to work here, what would you tell them that they had to do in order to get ahead?" What we learned in this part of the audit was a little disturbing, actually. We thought we already had a customer-focused organization, but in interviewing more than a hundred people in the organization, we heard the word "customer" just twice. In our employees' minds, pleasing the customer had little to do with getting ahead in the company.

Third, we engaged an outside firm to conduct focus groups involving more than 150 employees throughout our organization. They asked many of the same questions as the cultural transformation team, but they took an objective, outside view.

Then we pulled the information from all three phases together and were able to discover the real rules of the game in our own organization. We could also discern the underlying assumptions that produced those rules. We learned, for instance, that information was power in the existing culture and that if employees wanted to get ahead, they became experts by hoarding information. What they alone knew made them important to the organization. That, of course, told us that we would have to change that rule, since one of our key strategies was to be the sharing of information throughout the organization.

We also learned that you can't plan an entire reengineering project in advance, because what you discover during the project changes your plan. Every change you design is a living rough draft, not a perfected process. Reengineering is an iterative process. The problems you encounter themselves lead to better solutions, which is why it's essential to attack change in manageable chunks. We also learned that in reengineering you have to reengineer both human and technical systems, not just one or the other, and it can't all happen at once.

At any given time, we'll have a number of projects in various stages of maturation. In building the new business model, for instance, we went through what we called a controlled test environment during the summer of 1991. We did some marketing campaigns and some customer-service prototype work to learn more about how our model would work in practice.

Then in the fall we kicked off a pilot program. We took forty thousand existing customers out of our regular system and put them under the care of a small pilot unit still operating off-line. We had built a PC-based system to support a customer-management team that's servicing those forty thousand customers right now. The team consists of ten customer service representatives, a marketer, an expert in the company operations, and an information systems person. Their collective job is to service those forty thousand customers.

To some degree, there is still a division of duties within the team in that we have some people who are more expert at service than they are at sales, but we're finding that team members are figuring out that marketing and service are really one and the same. The service people are becoming marketers, and the marketers are on the phones servicing customers.

That is the beauty of this pilot approach. It lets us test our ideas on real customers using real employees without making us bet the farm that everything is going to work exactly as we thought it would.

We also have a pilot market-management team that is experimenting with the new ways of marketing that we've designed. That team is actually conducting campaigns, building strategic alliances with vendors and, more importantly, testing the interaction between the top and the bottom half of the figure eight.

We have also attacked several areas of what was the old factory. We have built the prototype of a reengineered application process, and we're about to operate it on a pilot basis, again using PCs. We have a life/health claims prototype that is almost ready to go on pilot, and a property/casualty prototype on the way, too.

The cultural audit that we did has made a big contribution to some major changes underway in human resources management—for instance, in the redesign of our promotion and reward system.

Our new philosophy is that we will reward for performance and promote on ability. In the old system, a promotion was a reward for having done a good job. That doesn't make sense. People should be rewarded for doing a good job. We'll do that with compensation. Promotion, on the other hand, should depend on people's ability to do the job to which they're being promoted, and it has little to do with their performance in the jobs they have now. So, we are redesigning the performance development program.

We've separated the results review and the performance development review. We give people their results review and adjust their compensation. Then, several months later, we conduct the performance development review. We separate the two reviews so that we can acknowledge and reward the results they turned in and still be clear about their need for additional growth and development. Promotion is not a reward, and by not treating it as such we hope to eliminate the Peter Principle in our company.

A measure of an employee's willingness to learn and develop as well as a measure of his or her ability to function in a team environment will be parts of our compensation mix. We're replacing the current job evaluation system that focuses on the performance of a single task with one that evaluates employee performance in developing a wider array of the more highly evolved skills that our business model demands. I guess this is pretty radical. We're going to pay people in part for the job they've done—for performance, in other words—and in part for getting ready to do the job we'll ask them to do in the future—for learning.

Also, in 1992 we launched a goal-sharing program that is different. Merit increases have always been awarded based on individual performance. This year we're cutting the individual merit increases by half. We tied the other half to team and corporate performance on all levels, not just for managers. In 1993, all normal merit raises will be based on team and corporate performance, and we will have a separate recognition program for individual stars. In general, we want the individual to prosper when the team and the corporation do.

Because we're reworking our training and development program and because we've placed a new priority on the wide and candid sharing of information, within two years we hope to be well along the way to establishing what I call a "thinking culture" in the company. By thinking culture, I mean a work environment in which employees, especially those closest to the customer, have the autonomy to make decisions and the training and information they need to make the right ones.

All together we have about ten separate reengineering projects underway right now, and they and the people operating them constitute what I call Company B. Company B is the new company that we're designing and building. Company A is the existing company. The interesting thing is that the people in Company A aren't waiting for their turn to get into the new stuff. They're saying that they want to operate as much as they can like the new prototypes within the limits of the old systems they have to use. Change breeds change, and we're finding that people want to jump on board because they see what's happening in Company B as the wave of the future.

None of this—building the new business models, operating the redesigned processes, or empowering our people—has happened without our employing new information technology, but in this area we still have some ground to cover. In the old assembly line environment, there was little need to share information through on-line systems, so investment in information systems lagged.

Our strategy to close the information gap centers on a three-year plan that will tie the development of our technology infrastructure to the development of our business models. We are working in partnership with our information systems staff, using their expertise as part of the development process instead of asking them for solutions once the process is set.

Together we'll create the customer-information channel that is central to our new business model. That channel has to provide easy to use work stations that deliver information in a format that meets users' needs and fosters sound decision-making. This open access to customer, product, and marketing information will allow employees to work in teams and to connect with other parts of the organization. We believe we're five years away from having the system we need, but it's a key priority. Information technology is the enabler for our new business model, because it will provide access to the information that is its fuel.

We were warned that reengineering was not something that was going to happen overnight, and we worried that if it did take four or five years to build the company we described in our vision that the people in the organization might grow impatient or lose heart. We also were concerned at first that if building the new company took us five years, it might be out of date before we finished. Now we know that neither concern is going to be a problem.

When you tackle the reengineering of an entire company by doing it in manageable chunks, people do see results, and the changes they see breed more change. When we get some short-term results, these results are advertised all over the company to say, "This is what change looks like." If you don't advertise and make a big deal of it, small changes can get lost. It's like when you're home all the time you don't see the changes in your kids, but go away for two weeks and when you get back you can't believe how much they've grown. In reengineering you have to make changes in chunks and show people what change looks like, because that's psychic income, which is the fuel that people need to keep on making changes.

As to the second concern, whether we were building a system that would be obsolete and irrelevant when it was done, we learned early on that we weren't building a monolith. We're building a flexible system in modular parts. If one part becomes irrelevant in a year, we can throw it away. If we can't build a system that we can keep changing over time, then we didn't do the right job up front with our vision.

The point most vividly illustrated by the DRG case is the power of vision—helping people to *see* what you mean. DRG used the figure eight. Since people learn through stories and pictures, this simple picture of what the company would be and how it would work was a powerful tool for communications within DRG.

DRG could have tried to reengineer without doing the extensive cultural assessment that it undertook, but the effort has paid off manyfold. What DRG learned about itself in that exercise turned out to be crucial in helping the company shape its reengineering strategy.

The DRG experience also clearly illustrates that reengineering must be an iterative process. It hardly ever proceeds straight ahead, one step at a time. Companies do not reengineer in a neat, orderly fashion. They start out with an overall vision and refine and modify it as they move toward it.

DRG made good use of pilots and proofs of concept in order to reduce the risk of the proposed changes. Any sane manager wants some assurance that what he or she proposes will work before betting the entire company—or an entire career—on it. Besides, pilots are useful teachers, too. Lessons learned in a pilot can send the reengineering team back for a bit more redesign before implementing the change across the entire company.

Finally, DRG's experience drives home the importance of paying attention to two elements that, if they are ignored, will short-circuit a reengineering process. One is the company's human resource and organizational infrastructure. The second is the company's information technology. Both are essential enablers of change. Neither represents the essence of reengineering, but both must support reengineering if it is to succeed.

CHAPTER 13

ONE COMPANY'S EXPERIENCE— BELL ATLANTIC

Bell Atlantic Corp., the Philadelphia-based, $12 billion communications company that serves the mid-Atlantic states, used to operate in a monopolistic world, free from competition. Accordingly, it responded to customers' requests according to its own timetable and without excessive regard for the quality of service it provided. Then Bell Atlantic's world changed. Now the company is changing, too—and at a breathtaking pace.

One of Bell Atlantic's principal businesses, making up 20 percent of its revenues and nearly half its corporate profits, involves providing carrier access services, or CAS. CAS is simply the link between Bell Atlantic's customers—residential and business— and their selected long-distance carriers, such as AT&T, Sprint, and MCI. Each of Bell Atlantic's seven regional operating companies had its own procedures for handling a carrier access request, but processing a request and hooking up the service typically took Bell Atlantic about fifteen days—and as much as thirty days for corporate customers needing a link for their high-speed data and video communications. As a monopoly provider, Bell Atlantic didn't have to care how long this process took.

Suddenly, Bell Atlantic discovered it needed to compete—but couldn't. Newcomers to the business built fiber-optic cables—a technology Bell Atlantic didn't yet have—in metropolitan areas where the Baby Bell had large corporate customers with heavy demands for voice, high-speed data, and video communications. The new companies could not only provide these customers with access service that was more reliable and less expensive than Bell Atlantic's, they could process service orders in a quarter of the time it took Bell Atlantic. It didn't take long for Bell Atlantic's biggest and most lucrative accounts to begin deserting for the competition.

Late in 1990, Regis Filtz, Bell Atlantic's newly appointed head of CAS, recognized the difference between his company's performance and that of the new competitors' and saw immediately that incremental change—making Bell Atlantic's performance a little better and a little faster—would fall far short of saving the company's business. In the spring of 1991, Filtz concluded that only reengineering would improve CAS service sufficiently to reverse the customer loss. In his words:

We needed dramatic improvements, and we needed them fast. Immediately after taking over CAS, I personally met with the three largest long-distance carriers to find out directly from them what they wanted from us, both short-term and long-term. The personal contact was very important, because it gave me information I wouldn't have gotten from marketing studies. For instance, I learned that while AT&T's official request was for a hookup within seven days, what they really wanted was service when they wanted it—in other words, on demand. And they wanted it with zero defects. MCI was asking us to reduce cycle times to one day.

With help from outside consultants, we did what I call a high-level analysis of our work processes—receiving and processing an order for [CAS] service, connecting the service, testing it, and turning it over to the customer. We found, among other things, that from start to finish there were at least thirteen handoffs among different work groups and that some twenty-seven different information systems were involved. Not only was the process slow, it was terribly expensive. Further study showed us that while the interval between receiving an order and turning the service over to the customer was fifteen days, our actual work time was only about ten hours. For a thirty-day interval, we did only about fifteen hours of work.

This high-level analysis showed us significant opportunities not only to reduce our process time dramatically, but also to slash our costs by a similar order of magnitude.

We had no time to waste, but we couldn't antagonize customers, so when we made a change we had to get it right. This wasn't something we could afford to do again and again to correct mistakes. So, we actually set up two different kinds of reengineering teams, one to come up with the ideas and the other to test and refine them in the real world.

The first team we called the core team. To head it, we selected a manager who had all the prerequisites I was looking for. She was respected by her peer group, and she was a good communicator, teacher, and role model. She could and would inspire others.

The core team leader's first job was to assemble a team of experts from among all the disciplines involved in the fragmented CAS process, being sure that they were competent in their skill areas and that they, too, were respected by their peers and were good communicators. The core team's job was to brainstorm, to redesign, and to blueprint the new process in detail. We gave them a goal. They were to find a way for Bell Atlantic to provide access services to customers in virtually zero cycle time.

We made their goal ambitious for three reasons: First, it's what our customers said they wanted in the long term. Second, meeting it would force a substantive change in the existing process, not just a fix. Third, we figured that zero cycle time was a level of performance that our competitors could never beat.

Frankly, the core team members were apprehensive. At first, they thought their task was impossible, and it took more than a little encouragement to get them to sign on, but they did. They began their work in mid-July of 1991, and within a month, they had designed a new process that physically pulled together under common supervision in one location all of the functions of the old process that had been geographically dispersed, separately managed, and spread among different departments.

As soon as we had a process design, we put the second team, which we called the lab team, to work. Their job was to test the core team's blueprinted design by using it to process real CAS orders. They would try the new process, change it however they liked, and then feed back their results to the core team. Thus, our reengineering process itself was iterative. The lab team became, in effect, a proto-type for the case team concept that our core team created.

The lab team was empowered to make whatever changes in work methods and procedures that were necessary to cut the process time, reduce expense, and produce a defect-free output. They were to discard all of the existing functional and departmental measure-ments and management objectives under which they used to work in their separate departments. Their only concern was figuring out how they could reduce cycle time, cut expense, and improve the quality of the output concurrently.

The lab team took over operational responsibility for servicing customers in a part of central Pennsylvania. Within several months, the team was working with cycle times measured in days instead of weeks. In some cases they had reduced them to hours. The quality of the service improved dramatically, too. Before the lab team began servicing that group of customers, we had four people working full time whose job was to track CAS orders that were not being com-pleted successfully. We have eliminated that group and saved more than $1 million a year on reworks in just that one location.

Currently we are extending the case team concept to all of Bell Atlantic's operating subsidiaries. The teams we're installing use the same process and process management systems that were used in the lab team's pilot. We've also identified the culture changes, the new job skills, and the revamped information systems that we'll need.

Bell Atlantic's management systems are being changed as well. We have been and are a hierarchical company that closely supervises individuals and measures their performance by internal criteria. We are moving toward self-managed and cross-functional work teams that are internally motivated to meet customer requirements, and to continuously improve cycle time, cut costs, and improve quality.

The culture and the values of the corporation are also changing. Under the old hierarchy, we could rely upon compliance to get results. With our redesigned processes, we have to rely on commit-ment. The difference is that in a compliance mode I do what I must do because my boss tells me I must do it. In a commitment mode, I understand what the corporation is trying to achieve and how we're going to achieve it, and I will do whatever it takes to make that happen, including changing the way I do my job if that is what is required.

We previously had individuals performing single functions with absolutely no knowledge of the entire system or of what happened to their work as it progressed downstream. We are moving toward a different arrangement in which tasks are combined, and we are creating systemic knowledge so that each of us understands the process as a whole, what our piece of it is, and how we can interact more effectively with others.

Even as we implement the case team concept, though, the core team is already working on the next iteration of reengineering, in which we will replace the case teams with *one* case worker and some new technology. Essentially, one person will be able to do what a team of people with different specialties does now. Instead of using a team to transcribe the elements of a customer order manually for each of our various systems, we have technology that will allow one person to take a customer's call and use his or her terminal to make electronically all the connections required to set up the service requested. When we reach this iteration, we will essentially be changing the order in which we respond to customer requests. We'll be setting up the service first and then taking the time to figure out how to bill and keep the records we need.

But that won't be the end of it. The final iteration as we see it now is self-provisioning, in which customers will interface directly with our system when they want the service. To the customer, it will seem as if it's working just the way the telephone system works today with routine voice calls. For us, there won't be any manual operations involved, and the cycle time will have become, in accordance with our goal, virtually zero.

As we reduce the cycle time toward zero, our labor costs appear to be dropping by an order of magnitude, from about $88 million to $6 million. Most important, we're keeping existing customers and attracting new ones.

As a matter of interest: We're already guaranteeing three-day installation on high-capacity digital circuits that used to need fifteen days or more. Three-day installation is currently the best interval offered in the industry, but in less than a year we expect to be able to provide the service within minutes in some selected locations.

After a little more than one year, the goal that seemed so impossible to us when we started is now within our grasp, and that certainly is much sooner than any of us imagined.

The people in charge of Bell Atlantic's process redesign understood reengineering well. First, they took cognizance of the fact that process redesign is not just about creating an abstract concept; the concept has to be made tangible. Second, they understood the importance of achieving dramatic results quickly and took the needed steps to accomplish that end.

Bell Atlantic used a core team to create redesign concepts and a lab team to test them in the field. The core team's job was to come up with breakthrough ideas. The lab team's job was to make them real. Whether a company uses two separate units connected by a feedback loop, as Bell Atlantic did, or a single reengineering team isn't important. It is only important that companies act on the understanding that process redesign is not an abstract endeavor. Ideas must be tested, and the organizational and human issues have to be factored into the new designs. Bell Atlantic's dual-team technique accomplished both these ends.

Another point that Bell Atlantic's experience illustrates is the usefulness of staged reengineering. The core team envisioned an ultimate objective of self-provisioning with no cycle time—that is, the company would give customers the ability to dial up the service they wanted instantaneously, much like any telephone user gets a long-distance line now: We dial "1," and it happens. But the Bell Atlantic team realized that they shouldn't try to reach this goal in a single leap. Doing so would take too long and require too great a capital investment. They decided instead to make the change in three steps, moving first to the case team, then to the case worker, and finally to self-provisioning. Each step yields a major improvement over the previous one, and each step sets the stage for the next one. In other words, Bell Atlantic achieved dramatic improvements fast, without compromising its ultimate goal.

It is also interesting to see how they attained those dramatic results. Bell Atlantic's first stage, when it moved to a case team, required little or no capital investment. The company used existing tools and mechanisms and even most of the existing people, but it broke down the organizational boundaries and organized the people around the process. Stage 1 required less capital investment and employee training than stage 2, which required a new computer system and people trained as case workers.

Finally, Bell Atlantic's second stage illustrates an interesting redesign technique: changing the order in which tasks are done. Traditionally, the company wouldn't connect a customer's service until it had collected all the information it needed or might need to perform all the tasks associated with providing the service—including billing. But in the second stage version of the reengineered process, case workers initiate service as soon as they have the information they need to do so. Billing information, which takes longer to collect, can be dealt with later. When the order of tasks is rearranged, as the Bell Atlantic case shows, customer waiting time can be cut substantially.

The experiences of these four companies in reengineering their business processes aren't typical, because no two companies and no two reengineering processes are alike. Readers can learn from others' successes, but they can't copy them exactly. No guaranteed-to-work prescriptions exist for reengineering. That doesn't mean, however, that there are no guidelines for success. There are, and they largely consist of ways not to fail, as we will see in the next chapter.

CHAPTER 14

SUCCEEDING AT REENGINEERING

Sadly, we must report that despite the success stories described in previous chapters, many companies that begin reengineering don't succeed at it. They end their efforts precisely where they began, making no significant changes, achieving no major performance improvement, and fueling employee cynicism with yet another ineffective business improvement program. Our unscientific estimate is that as many as 50 percent to 70 percent of the organizations that undertake a reengineering effort do not achieve the dramatic results they intended.

Nonetheless, while we say reengineering is often unsuccessful, it is not a high-risk endeavor. This apparent oxymoron isn't oxymoronic at all. Consider the difference in risk between roulette and chess. Roulette is a high-risk endeavor; chess is not, although a player may lose at chess as frequently as at roulette. Roulette is purely a game of chance. Once the money is put down, players have no control over the outcome; in chess, chance plays no part in the outcome. The better player can expect to win; loss results from ability and strategy.

As with chess, so with reengineering: The key to success lies in knowledge and ability, not in luck. If you know the rules and avoid making mistakes, you're extremely likely to succeed. In reengineering, moreover, the same mistakes get made over and over. The first step to reengineering success, therefore, is to recognize these common failures and learn to avoid them.

The Russian chess champion Sergei Tartakower once said of a chess board that was set up for a game, "The mistakes are all there, waiting to be made." What follows is a catalogue of the most common errors that lead companies to fail at reengineering. Avoid them, and you almost can't help but get it right.

• Try to fix a process instead of changing it

The most egregious way to fail at reengineering is by not reengineering at all, but rather conducting process changes and just calling it reengineering. Recently the term "reengineering" has acquired a certain cachet, and it has been attached to all kinds of programs that in fact have nothing to do with radical process redesign. We find it useful to recall the old saying that hanging a sign on a cow that says "I am a horse" doesn't make it a horse.

We described in Chapter 2 how IBM Credit Corporation reengineered its credit issuance process. However, we neglected to say that IBM Credit first tried to "fix" the old process several times before it faced up to the need for radical process redesign.

The company first attempted to automate the existing process, using computer technology to speed up the information flows and task performance. Automation consisted of giving the specialists on-line computer terminals into which they could type the results of their individual efforts. They still did their work on their respective departments' own, off-line computers, and each deal was still handled serially—first by credit, then by business practices, then by pricing, and so on. The paper application forms continued to travel from department to department. In fact, the only benefit that this automation brought to IBM Credit was that it enabled the specialists who performed the final step (quote letter preparation) to extract the results of the previous steps of the process from the on-line system. In trying to automate its operations, IBM Credit managed only to immortalize a bad process by committing it to computer software, making it even more difficult to alter in the future.

Dissatisfied with the paltry performance improvement obtained from automation, the company next attempted a whole stable of business improvement techniques. It tried using queuing theory and linear programming techniques to balance the work across the various departments to minimize wait times. The results proved insignificant. The company set performance standards for each step in the process; when it later measured employees' actual results, it found that they were achieving nearly 100 percent compliance with the standards, but turnaround times had grown longer still. How to account for this anomalous result? It turned out that when pressed for time, people conveniently discovered errors on bid requests they were handling, which entitled them to send these back to the preceding department for rework, thereby excluding that request from their measurements.

IBM Credit's experience is not atypical. Organizations often go to great trouble and expense to avoid the radical redesign associated with reengineering. They may reorganize, which means that they don't change work processes at all, only the administrative boxes around the people doing it. Companies downsize, which just means using fewer people to do the same or less work in the same way. Companies try motivational programs, which use incentives to try to get people to work harder.

Existing processes, even if they're the source of a company's business problems, are nonetheless familiar; the organization is comfortable with them. The infrastructure to support them is already in place. Improving them seems so much easier and more "sensible" than throwing them out and starting all over. Incrementalism is the path of least resistance for most organizations. It is also the surest way to fail at reengineering.

• Don't focus on business processes

Not long ago, the progressive management of the U.S. subsidiary of a major European company commissioned several task forces of workers to address the critical issues of the day: empowerment, teamwork, innovation, customer service, and so on. The task forces' agendas were a lexicon of contemporary business clichés. Each group was given ninety days to develop recommendations as to how the organization could make major progress on its respective issue. The teams received *carte blanche*; no idea would be considered off limits or too wild. The task forces worked intensively for ninety days and produced precisely nothing. To be sure, they submitted reams of paper full of platitudinous recommendations, but all who read them understood immediately that these meant nothing and that nothing would come of them.

Why did this effort, with so much executive support and widespread participation, end in such failure? Because the problems were poorly defined. "Teamwork" and "empowerment" are abstractions and generalities around which it's impossible to get one's arms. They describe characteristics or attributes that one might want an organization to exhibit, but there is no direct way to achieve them. They are *consequences* of process designs and they can only be achieved in that context. How is one supposed to begin working on empowerment if not through the architecture of the work processes? "Innovation" is also the result of well-designed processes, not a thing in itself. The flaw in this company's efforts, and in similar attempts elsewhere, is that it failed to take a process perspective on the business. Without that, business improvement efforts amount to rearranging deck chairs on the *Titanic*.

• Ignore everything *except* process redesign

A reengineering effort, as we have seen, triggers changes of many kinds. Job designs, organizational structures, management systems—everything associated with the process—must be refashioned in order to maintain a coherent business system diamond.

As we related in Chapter 2, when Ford reengineered its vendor payment process, the effects reached as far as clerks on the receiving dock, who suddenly became decision makers. Instead of just stamping paper with times and dates, they now had to use a computer terminal to determine whether the arriving shipment corresponded to an outstanding order. If not, it was their responsibility to refuse the shipment and send it back. People who formerly had virtually no responsibilities now had to think and make decisions.

At IBM Credit, people who previously knew only how to check credit are now evaluating and pricing entire financing deals. To do this, they not only had to learn new jobs, they had to acquire new attitudes about their jobs.

Capital Holding's Direct Response Group (DRG) rethought its entire approach to the customer and reengineered many processes. As a consequence, DRG had to redesign its job-rating schemes, compensation policies, career paths, recruitment and training programs, promotion policies—practically every management system, in other words—in order to support the new process designs.

Even managers who are anxious for radical process redesign are often frightened by the full range of changes that such redesigns necessitate. We often encounter the following scenario: A senior manager commissions a reengineering team to produce breakthrough improvements for a troublesome process. Some time later the team returns, describes a breakthrough concept, and shows how it will eliminate 90 percent of the cycle time, 95 percent of the cost, and 99 percent of the errors. The manager squirms with joy. The team then proceeds to explain how the redesigned process will require a new job rating system, the consolidation of numerous departments, the redefinition of management authority, and a different style of labor relations. The senior manager squirms again, but not with joy. "I asked you to reduce costs and errors," he or she says, "not to remake the company." The team then is usually disbanded and its breakthrough concept never heard from again. But remaking the company is precisely what reengineering is about.

• Neglect people's values and beliefs

People need some reason to perform well within the reengineered processes. It isn't enough simply to put new processes in place; managers must motivate employees to rise to the challenge of these processes by supporting the new values and beliefs the processes demand. In other words, management must pay attention to what goes on in people's heads as well as what happens on their desks.

When Ford reengineered the way it paid its vendors, workers' attitudes and behaviors had to shift as well. Purchasing personnel could no longer view vendors as adversaries to be beaten down. They had to be viewed as Ford's partners in a shared business process.

When DRG reengineered its process for reviewing insurance applications, it also had to make a radical change in its culture. Supervisors could no longer be taskmasters, but had to function as providers of service to the employees actually performing the work—making sure that case workers had all the tools and support they needed to do their jobs.

Changes that require shifts in attitude are not easily accepted. Merely giving speeches isn't sufficient. New management systems must cultivate the required values by rewarding behavior that exhibits them. But senior managers must also give speeches about these new values, as well as demonstrate their commitment to them by their personal behavior.

• Be willing to settle for minor results

Big results require big ambitions. A critical test of ambition occurs at that point in a reengineering effort when someone suggests that a modest change will make the process work 10 percent better for practically no cost, in contrast to the pain and suffering engendered by reengineering. The temptation to take the easy path and to settle for the marginal improvement is great. In the long run, however, marginal improvement is no improvement at all, but a detriment.

Marginal improvements, as a rule, further complicate the current process, making it subsequently more difficult to figure out how things really work. Even worse, making additional investments of time or capital into an existing process only discourage management from dumping that process down the road. Most perniciously, taking incremental steps further reinforces a culture of incrementalism, creating a company with no valor or courage.

• Quit too early

It should not be surprising that some companies abandon reengineering or scale back their reengineering goals at the first sign of a problem. They lose their nerve. But we've also seen companies call off their reengineering effort at the first sign of success. As soon as they have something to show for all their pain and suffering they stop. The initial success becomes an excuse to return to the easy life of business as usual. In either case, by failing to persevere the company forgoes the huge payoffs down the road.

• Place prior constraints on the definition of the problem and the scope of the reengineering effort

A reengineering effort is doomed to fail when, before it even begins, corporate management narrowly defines the problem to be solved or limits its scope. Defining the problem and establishing its scope are steps in the reengineering effort itself. Reengineering begins with articulating the objectives that the effort seeks to achieve, not the ways in which these objectives will be met.

The experience of an industrial equipment manufacturer illustrates the point. Senior management told its consultants that the company's order fulfillment process was too expensive. Their charge was to shrink the operating cost of this process.

As the consultants investigated the problem, they talked to the company's customers, all of whom said that they hated practically everything about the company except the equipment it made. If they could buy those same products from someone else, they said, they would do so in a minute.

The higher-ups, insulated from direct contact with their market, thought the problem was the internal cost of order fulfillment, but it really lay in the entire customer service process—fulfillment, support, and communications. Everything in the interface with the customer was broken. Had the consultants accepted their charge at face value and limited themselves to examining the cost of the process, as an internal reengineering team commissioned by management might have been constrained to do under the circumstances, they would not have discovered the real nature of the company's difficulties.

It isn't uncommon for managers at senior levels of large organizations to be so out of touch with customer or production reality that they don't know just how broken some of their business processes are. Insulated from the process level, senior management isn't equipped to define the problem to be solved nor to delimit its scope.

It's also common for companies to state that the target is a business process but then proceed to restrict the reengineering effort to an arbitrary and small segment of the process that happens to fit neatly within existing organizational boundaries. This course is a sure-fire recipe for failure. Reengineering must break boundaries, not reinforce them. Reengineering must feel disruptive, not comfortable.

Insisting that reengineering be neat is insisting that it not be reengineering.

• Allow existing corporate cultures and management attitudes to prevent reengineering from getting started

A company's prevailing cultural characteristics can inhibit or defeat a reengineering effort before it begins. For instance, if a company operates by consensus, its people will find the top-down nature of reengineering an affront to their sensibilities. Companies whose short-term orientations keep them exclusively focused on quarterly results may find it difficult to extend their vision to reengineering's longer horizons. Organizations with a bias against conflict may be uncomfortable challenging long-established rules. It is executive management's responsibility to anticipate and overcome such barriers.

• Try to make reengineering happen from the bottom up

It is axiomatic that reengineering never, ever happens from the bottom up. There are two reasons why frontline employees and middle managers are unable to initiate and implement a successful reengineering effort, no matter how great the need or how prodigious their talent.

The first reason that the push for reengineering must come from the top of an organization is that people near the front lines lack the broad perspective that reengineering demands. Their expertise is largely confined to the individual functions and departments that they inhabit. They may see very clearly—probably better than anyone else—the narrow problems from which their departments suffer, but it is difficult for them to see a process as a whole and to recognize its poor overall design as the source of their problems. Frontline managers embrace incrementalism more readily than reengineering because they can act incrementally without exceeding the range of their vision.

Second, any business process inevitably crosses organizational boundaries, so no mid-level manager will have sufficient authority to insist that such a process be transformed. Its scope will inevitably transcend his or her domain of responsibility. Furthermore, some of the affected middle managers will correctly fear that dramatic changes to existing processes might diminish their own power, influence, and authority. These managers have much invested in the existing ways of doing things, and the future of the company may be implicitly—and sometimes explicitly—compromised by their own career interests. They fear change, because the new rules aren't clear. If radical change threatens to bubble up from below, they may resist it and throttle it. Only strong leadership from above will induce these people to accept the transformations that reengineering brings.

• Assign someone who doesn't understand reengineering to lead the effort

Senior management leadership is a necessary prerequisite for successful reengineering, but not just any senior manager will do. The leader must be someone who understands reengineering and is viscerally committed to it. The leader must also be someone who is oriented toward operations and appreciates the relationship between operational performance and financial results. Only a process-oriented senior executive, who is capable of thinking about the entire value-added chain—from product concept to sales and service—can lead a reengineering effort. Seniority and authority are not enough; understanding and the right mindset are critical as well.

• Skimp on the resources devoted to reengineering

The laws of thermodynamics say that you can't get something for nothing. In our context, that means a company cannot achieve the performance breakthroughs that reengineering promises without investing in its reengineering program. The most important component of this investment is the time and attention of the company's best people. Reengineering cannot be entrusted to the semi-competent, the hangers-on with nothing better to do.

Reengineering also demands the direct and personal involvement of senior management. Just as it cannot bubble up from the bottom of the organization, reengineering cannot be delegated down into it. Senior people don't have to do the reengineering themselves. They can deputize helpers and collaborators, but they cannot abdicate the responsibility for the effort to them. Reengineering must be the leader's personal project, with all that it implies. Quarterly progress reviews won't do. The senior management team must invest regular effort in guiding and monitoring the activities of all the reengineering projects underway in the company.

Assigning skimpy resources to the reengineering effort also signals the organization that management doesn't consider the attempt to be terribly important and encourages people to ignore or resist it in the expectation that before long it will have run its course and gone away.

• Bury reengineering in the middle of the corporate agenda

We tell companies that if they don't put reengineering at the top of their agenda, they should leave it off entirely. If management attention and energy are spread across many different efforts or programs, of which reengineering is only one, reengineering will not get the intense attention that it requires. Without constant management concern, resistance and inertia—the natural tendency of people and organizations to continue doing pretty much what they have always done—will bring the effort to a halt. Only if people recognize that management is committed to reengineering, is concentrating on it, and is giving it regular and close attention, will they reconcile themselves to its inevitability.

• Dissipate energy across a great many reengineering projects

Reengineering requires sharp focus and enormous discipline, which is another way of saying that companies must concentrate their reengineering efforts on a small number of processes at any given time. An organization becomes bewildered rather than energized when it's asked to do too much at once. The customer service, research and development, and sales processes may all need radical redesign, but nothing is likely to happen if a company tries to tackle them all simultaneously unless it has exceptional management capacity. Management's time and attention are limited, and reengineering won't obtain the crucial support it needs if managers have to flit among projects.

• Attempt to reengineer when the CEO is two years from retirement

The CEO or business unit head who is a year or two away from retiring may take a dim and unenthusiastic view of reengineering. This isn't because he or she has grown lazy or no longer cares about the organization's future. Rather, making fundamental changes in business processes will inevitably have major consequences for the structure of the company and many of its management systems. An imminent retiree may simply not want to deal with such complex issues or to make commitments that will constrain a successor.

A second problem raised by a CEO close to retirement is the effect that the impending change at the top is likely to have on other managers. Especially in hierarchical organizations, contenders for a senior post that is about to open up often feel that they are being watched and judged. If so, they may be more interested in individual performance than in being part of a large, collective reengineering effort. Furthermore, they'll have no interest in any program that changes the familiar rules by which they've gained their positions in the organization, and they will want to avoid any possible risk until the succession die is cast.

Beware of CEOs who, near retirement, contend that they are

now ready to accept the risks that reengineering entails. "After all," a chief executive may argue, "I have little to lose at this late stage in my career." True, but if they have waited until now to become bold executive managers, they may not, in a short period of time, be able to learn how to behave in the way the rule requires.

• Fail to distinguish reengineering from other business improvement programs

One problem from which many companies—regrettably—don't suffer is a dearth of business change programs. As times get tougher, purported panaceas proliferate. The business media are brimming over with ideas and programs to make companies better: quality improvement, strategic alignment, "rightsizing," customer-supplier partnerships, innovation, and empowerment, to name a few. Usually these programs are ephemeral. As one corporate wag told us, "Every month, our senior management goes to some seminar and comes home with a new religion. We just hold our breath until they get over it." A danger for reengineering is that employees will see it as just another Program of the Month. This danger will certainly materialize if reengineering is delegated to an impotent staff group. To preclude this possibility, management must make reengineering the responsibility of line managers, not of staff specialists. Moreover, if the company is in fact seriously committed to another business improvement program (such as TQM), then great care must be taken to carefully position reengineering relative to the other program. Otherwise, confusion will result and enormous energy will be expended on pointless internecine warfare about which program is superior.

• Concentrate exclusively on design

Reengineering isn't just about redesign. It's also about translating new designs into reality. The difference between winners and losers at reengineering doesn't usually lie in the quality of their respective ideas, but in what they do with them. With the losers, reengineering never moves beyond the idea phase into implementation.

• Try to make reengineering happen without making anybody unhappy

The aphorism about the need to break eggs to make omelets is very applicable to reengineering. It would be nice to say that reengineering is a win-win program that leaves everyone better off; it would be nice, but it would also be a lie. Reengineering isn't to everyone's advantage. Some employees do have a vested interest in current operations, some people will lose their jobs, and some workers may be uncomfortable with their jobs post-reengineering. Trying to please everyone is a hopeless ambition that will either devalue reengineering to a program of incremental change or delay its implementation into the future.

• Pull back when people resist making reengineering's changes

That people resist change shouldn't surprise anyone, especially not those in charge of a company's reengineering effort. Resistance is an inevitable reaction to major change. The first step in managing resistance, however, is to expect it and not let it set the effort back.

We have heard some managers say that reengineering failed in their companies because people resisted change. This is like saying that Newton's Second Law—a body in motion tends to stay in motion—is a major cause of automobile accidents. It isn't Newton's Law, but people's failure to heed it that causes crashes, and management's failure to anticipate and plan for the inevitable resistance that reengineering will encounter is the true cause of its failure.

• Drag the effort out

Reengineering is stressful for everyone in a company, and stretching it over a long time period extends the discomfort. Our experience suggests that twelve months should be long enough for a company to move from articulation of a case for action to the first field release of a reengineered process. Take longer, and people will become impatient, confused, and distracted. They will conclude that reengineering is another bogus program and the effort will fall apart.

Undoubtedly, there are more paths that lead to reengineering failure than those we have just listed. People are remarkably resourceful in finding new ways to drop the ball. However, one strong thread runs through all the pitfalls that we have encountered. That thread is the role of senior management. If reengineering fails, no matter what the proximate cause, the underlying reason can invariably be traced to senior managers' inadequate understanding or leadership of the reengineering effort. Reengineering is always born in the executive suite. All too often, it dies there as well.

Despite the opportunities for failure, we are heartened by the many successes of reengineering. Organizations that approach reengineering with understanding, commitment, and strong executive leadership *will* succeed at it. The payoffs of successful reengineering are spectacular—for the individual company, for its managers and its employees, and for the American economy as a whole. The time for hesitation is gone; the time for action is now.

EPILOGUE

Despite their well-publicized difficulties, American businesses are not yet an endangered species. Those that we cite throughout this book are themselves proof that American companies can change to compete in the evolving world economy. They have learned that an enviable reputation, good financial controls, and a debt-free balance sheet no longer guarantee survival. Surviving in today's world demands strong executive leadership, an intense focus on customers and their needs, and superior process design and execution. Reengineering is one of the tools companies must possess and know how to use to acquire those prerequisites to success.

In the last decade, many miracle cures have been prescribed for the ills of American business. Most of them have passed through the patients without discernible effect.

Reengineering, in contrast, promises no miracle cure. It offers no quick, simple, and painless fix. On the contrary, it entails difficult, strenuous work. It requires that people running companies and working in them change how they think as well as what they do. It requires that companies replace their old practices with entirely new ones. Doing so isn't easy. It cannot be accomplished with motivational lectures and catchy wall posters.

Although we have explored reengineering at some length, we have barely scratched the surface of the topic, as readers who attempt reengineering in their own companies will discover. For instance, we have written only a little about how organizations can actually make reengineering happen. A methodology for conducting a reengineering effort, the orchestration of the change campaign, the design and timing of releases of newly-redesigned processes, and tactics for dealing with the most common problems that arise in implementation are issues that go beyond the scope of a single book.

Moreover, other important questions about reengineering as yet have no conclusive answers. For example, "What impact will the reengineering of American companies have on the U.S. economy?" And how will reengineering's flattening of corporate hierarchies affect managers and executives accustomed to gauging their self-worth by their positions within an organization?

The uncertainties of reengineering, however, cannot be used as an excuse to put off what must be done. Leading corporations in nearly every industry have already begun to reengineer. As more companies bring their key processes up to higher levels of performance, the reengineering option becomes a competitive necessity for others in the same industry. Reengineering by even one key participant in a market creates a new benchmark level that all competitors must meet.

Reengineering is still a new endeavor; all of us engaged in it are pioneers. The world of the industrial revolution is giving way to an era of a global economy, powerful information technologies, and relentless change. The curtain is rising on the Age of Reengineering. Those who respond to its challenges will write the new rules of American business. All that is needed is the will to succeed and the courage to begin.

INDEX